GREAT
BIRD PAINTINGS
OF THE WORLD

VOLUME I
THE OLD MASTERS

Christine E. Jackson

ANTIQUE COLLECTORS' CLUB

ACKNOWLEDGEMENTS

My special thanks are due to Andrew B Jackson for many hours of patient scrutiny of paintings while assisting me with their choice and later with the identification of the bird species. I also wish to thank Maureen and Lionel Lambourne for their interest in this book and for sharing their considerable knowledge of paintings worldwide. I am particularly grateful to Rafael Valls and Emma Millett of the gallery Rafael Valls Limited in Duke Street, London, who have been a great support both in allowing me to see paintings and use photographs, and in their kindly interest in the book throughout its compilation. I thank Richard Green and Christopher Gibbs of London, and Galerie Edel in Cologne for generously allowing us to reproduce paintings in their galleries and Bridgeman Art Library and The Courtauld Institute of Art for permission to reproduce their photographs.

© 1993 Christine E. Jackson
World copyright reserved

ISBN 1 85149 178 3

Other books by Christine E. Jackson:

British Names of Birds, 1968
Bird Illustrators: some artists in early lithography, 1975
Collecting Bird Stamps, 1977
Wood Engravings of Birds, 1978
Bird etchings: the illustrators and their books 1655-1855, 1985
Prideaux John Selby: a gentleman naturalist, 1992

Frontispiece : Parrots *by Frans Snyders (see pages 64-65)*

British Library Cataloguing-in-Publication Data
A catalogue record for this book is available from the British Library.

Printed in England by Antique Collectors' Club Ltd,
Woodbridge, Suffolk, IP12 1DS
on Consort Royal Satin paper from Donside Mills, Aberdeen

LIST OF ILLUSTRATIONS

FOREWORD

In the Sixth Book of *The Aeneid*, Virgil wrote the famous line: 'Easy is the descent into Hell.' 'Facilis descensus Averno.'

Avernus was Virgil's portal to Hades, a noxious lake in the Italian Campania where fumes from the fetid waters were supposed to kill all the birds that flew over it or frequented the shore. The lake received its name from the Greek *aornos* – *a* in Greek meaning not and *ornos* or *ornis*, a bird. Hell was construed as a place without birds; a world without birds would be hell.

Consciously, or subconsciously this seems to have been a philosophical underpinning of countless civilisations both east and west, primitive and modern. Nowhere is this mystical kinship more evident than in the vast opus of what we refer to as western art. The number of paintings in which a bird plays a role is beyond counting. In fact, 'bird watching', through the impetus of this series, may well become a new indoor sport.

A distinction can be made between a painting with a bird in it, and a bird-painting. Contemporary wild-life art has tipped the balance towards the latter – that is, paintings of birds in their own right. During the period covered by this first volume, Christine Jackson has shown through her scholarly research, the role of the individual birds in the paintings was frequently more than just aesthetic. Religious art was filled with allegorical messages, and the use of birds to emphasise the patron's social status or occupation was not uncommon.

In short, birds and animals in general were depicted in the service of man, as nutritional, sporting, spiritual, economic and social appendages to the human condition. In these guises the paintings would not qualify as bird paintings, rather they are paintings with birds in them. Scientific correctness, therefore, was not as important as it would have been had the paintings been of birds in their own right. From the post-photographic perspective of the twentieth century, many of the birds – especially birds in flight – are 'inaccurate'.

Although our sensitivities towards the natural world may have evolved over the intervening years, the aesthetic appeal of birds is shared with generations past. Society in general and artists in particular saw birds in a different light, and in different roles. This in no way invalidates the bird art of the Old Masters nor the message which, on the wings of their birds, has crossed the centuries.

David M. Lank, FRSA
September 1993

Opposite: The Element of Air *(detail) by Jan Brueghel (see pages 40 and 41).*

INTRODUCTION

From the earliest pictorial records, we know that men have been fascinated by birds. Artists have attempted to capture the spirit and beauty of birds by painting them on cave and tomb walls, by carving their images on bone, and shaping their forms in mosaics, from time immemorial. The aesthetic pleasure derived from birds was additional to gastronomic delights and their value as suppliers of eggs and feathers. But above all, birds can fly and men have always aspired to fly. Their ability to take wing has been a source of wonder and envy, transmuted into birds being the emblem of the soul.

Man's different attitudes to birds are reflected in bird paintings. They are the subjects of falconry and shooting; the emblems of the soul capable of soaring above this world; and the sharers of our earthly world with all its variety of scenery. Sometimes the approach is scientific by careful recording of the birds' physical form, at others it is anthropomorphic when birds are made to appear to act like humans. Whatever the reasons for an attempt to portray them, birds attract us because they are so beautiful.

Centuries passed before man learned to use oil-based paints, first on panels of wood, then canvas. Fourteen centuries Anno Domini, to be precise, before this medium was first fully appreciated in Europe where, at that time, every part of a man's life was dominated by religion. Easel art was born into the service of the Roman Catholic Church. The whole of art belonged primarily to the church where stained glass windows, mosaics, tapestries, sculpture, paintings and illuminated religious texts all served to illustrate the Christian faith.

Within this context, artists who wished to paint birds adapted their art to suit the situation. The church used many symbols or icons to get the Christian message across to a largely illiterate congregation. Saints had icons, many of them birds. Saint John the Evangelist was instantly recognised as being St John by his attendant eagle. Several hundred Madonnas showed the Christ child holding a goldfinch, a symbol of his passion, in his hand, while a dove hovered overhead representing the Holy Spirit. These emblems are widely recognised, but there were dozens more whose significance is no longer certainly known.

For some strange reason, the church also allowed artists to paint historical and classical subjects, even though these pagan subjects were sometimes immoral. Much of Europe had been under Greek and Roman rule, so the ancient myths, with gods and goddesses also having their own emblematic birds, Zeus's eagle and Juno's peacock to name just the supreme god and goddess, were well known and their iconography recognised. Many more birds became symbols of good qualities, or evil. All were expertly and legitimately used by artists who had a great desire to paint birds. The deeply devout Roman Catholic, Rubens, painted *Ganymede and the Eagle* (pages 46-47), as well as the figures of Adam and Eve in *The Garden of Eden* by Brueghel.

With the freeing of the Netherlands from the Spanish yoke in the sixteenth century, Protestantism spread and flourished. Artists no longer worked exclusively on a large scale to adorn churches and on a smaller scale to embellish sacred texts, and the close links between church and state were loosened. Even in Italy, the heart of catholicism, Renaissance men acquired a new outlook, with a great curiosity about themselves as part of nature, and the animals and plants that were an integral part of their world. Birds, outside the iconography and symbolic pattern of religion, were now drawn and enjoyed for their own intrinsic worth. No longer was it necessary to paint *Noah's Ark* or *The Garden of Eden* (pages 34-39) in order to include animals in the picture. There was an intermediary period, where the ark was still present, but relegated to the background with the main interest in the foreground where the animals were grouped and any human figures were tending them, as the work of Jan Brueghel and the Bassano family demonstrates. By the mid-seventeenth century, even this was unnecessary, and birds were placed in the fore-, mid- and background of paintings called *A Concert of Birds, Assembly of Birds* or *Birds in a Landscape.*

At this same time, all the attitudes of man to birds were once again being represented, though they now formed the main motif. Many falconry and hunting scenes were painted, often with the trophies of the chase piled in a prominent position. The still life painting became popular almost at the same time as the freedom to paint birds alive irrespective of religious content in the picture. In the religious paintings there had been carefully painted still life elements, such as household vessels and food on tables (including poultry and fish) but now these everyday objects were painted independently, for their own beauty of texture, colour and shape. Among the earliest still life paintings was the dead partridge by Jacopo de' Barbari painted in 1504. He also painted what is regarded as the first live still life bird painting in oils, *A Sparrowhawk* (pages 20-21). The skill of these early painters to catch the spirit and character of the bird, not only its physical shape and colours, is truly remarkable.

The proportion of still life bird paintings to live bird paintings is far higher than the balance of plates in this book suggests. Our present-day taste does not favour dead bird pictures, or, rather, it is currently a minority taste. However, the opportunity to have a perfectly still bird which the artist could arrange to show the texture of all parts of the plumage, attracted many fine artists to this genre and produced some outstandingly skilful and beautiful bird paintings. Snyders, Weenix and Fyt are the best-known exponents of animal still life painting, usually with dead birds and mammals together with guns and powder horns. We have chosen examples from Snyders' and Fyt's equally good paintings of live birds. One outstanding example, that has been excluded owing to lack of space, is the *Two Dead Waxwings* by Lukas Cranach, but there are many more artists of the German school working close to Dürer, who painted watercolour studies of birds.

Frans van Cuyck, Still-life with Bittern *(see pages 118 and 119).*

Frans van Mieris, Lady in a Red Jacket Feeding a Parrot *(see pages 106 and 107).*

Before easel oil paintings were made possible c.1430, many watercolour studies of birds were made. These were usually preparatory sketches for birds that were to be included in tapestries or frescoes. Watercolours continued to be used for detailed studies of birds, and since they were more quickly executed, often used to record newly imported, exotic birds that might not survive for long. Spanish, Portuguese and then Dutch ships, trading in the east and west, brought home many exciting, brilliantly plumaged birds never seen before in Europe. They came from newly colonised parts of Africa, Asia and South America. These rarities first found their way into the menageries of emperors and kings who commanded their artists to record them. Watercolours were more suitable for this purpose, for subtlety of colouring and fine feathering were better reproduced by the fine brushes used for watercolour painting. Miniaturists, such as Nicolas Robert (page 78-79), used to working in great detail, were ideally suited for this work.

As the number of exotics grew, so the number painted on canvas, as ornamental pieces to decorate the walls of large houses, became popular. The finest artists were employed by wealthy owners of menageries, lesser talents had to be content with native bird species, barnyard and village pond inhabitants. Even exotic parrots, however, soon became so numerous in Holland and Flanders that they appeared in paintings of the interiors of homes of quite modest citizens. These paintings were commissioned by wealthy merchants, and it was they who also preferred other genre paintings of flowers, fruits, insects, and, of course, birds.

With the increase in commerce and the tremendous growth in prosperity in the Netherlands, many of the Dutch and Flemish artists were sponsored to travel to Italy to complete their artistic training. On their return, they painted birds in classical landscapes with the beautiful blue skies and glowing yellow light of Italy, that so captured the imagination of the Low Countries' painters that they nearly all adopted these features, even those who had never set foot in Italy. However extraordinary the combination of common mallards with peacocks and macaws, flat Low Countries marshland scenery, a classical urn and Italian sky, somehow these disparate elements became blended into some of the most beautiful, skilfully painted bird pictures of all time. The plates in this book represent the work of early master painters who produced some of the world's greatest bird pictures.

The evolution of bird art, from the 1430s up to 1699, is a complex weave of religious and secular painting, the development of different genre paintings, the interaction between different schools of painting, and the changing perception of nature by post-Renaissance men. Add to this mix the astonishing array of new bird species being discovered and brought to Europe at a time when there was a great awakening of scientific interest in the world around them by seventeenth century artists and naturalists, and it is no wonder that birds figured so largely in the Golden Age of Dutch and Flemish painting. As far as bird art is concerned, it found its pinnacle of achievement in Melchior de Hondecoeter, the greatest painter of bird pictures until the nineteenth century.

There is currently great interest in searching early paintings for the plants and animals to be found on the 'forest floor'. One of the additional pleasures for ornithologists when walking round art galleries, is to search, not just the floor, but the 'tree tops' of a wide range of paintings.

An astonishing number of different bird species may be discovered, even in religious paintings of the mid-fifteenth century. Apart from scores of European birds, newly imported birds aroused so much interest that they were carefully, if unobtrusively, placed in the sky or perched on branches of trees in scenes of the annunciation, the nativity, or Madonnas with the

Christ child, or, for example, *St John at Patmos* (page 24-25). The first record of the presence in Italy, Germany and the Low Countries of some South American and East Indian birds is to be found in fourteenth and fifteen century religious paintings. Some of these birds later became symbolic, but many are there purely for decorative purposes or for sheer delight in a colourful, hitherto unknown bird.

Portraits are another source worth scrutinizing. Early family portraits, such as the Hans Eworth (c.1520-74) painting of William Brooke, 10th Baron Cobham, with his wife and six children, often include family pets. His children are shown holding a dog, a monkey and a goldfinch, while on the dinner table is a blue-fronted amazon parrot, perhaps the first to be seen in England. Van Dyck painted a fine portrait of the Balbi boys with their most unusual pets, two choughs. Portraits of princes are often accompanied by magnificent birds of prey, and these are complemented by paintings of small aristocratic girls holding a finch or standing alongside an exotic, larger pet bird. Later, women's portraits were painted showing them feeding a parrot, usually an African grey parrot.

The first plate in this book is an example of this kind of bird-spotting in galleries. Van Eyck has created a truly great piece of bird painting within *The Madonna with Canon George van der Paele*. Though we cannot regard these pictures as bird paintings because the birds form such a small part of the design, nevertheless, the birds increase our enjoyment of these works of art, just as our gardens are enlivened and enhanced by the presence of live birds. In addition, from the sixteenth century onwards, these portraits of live birds are frequently very beautifully and realistically painted at a time when bird book illustrators, supposedly working on scientifically accurate reproductions of birds for identification purposes, could only reproduce stiff figures drawn from stuffed models. The Nicolas Robert *Blue Peacock Displaying* (pages 78-79) and Kessel's birds (pages 94-95) were painted from stuffed specimens, and these have been included for comparison with the live birds painted in de Hondecoeter's pictures. Robert's and Kessel's birds were great bird paintings for their time, but the difference is that de Hondecoeter's birds are great bird paintings for all and every time. Paintings of birds were far superior to illustrations of birds, from the fifteenth to the middle of the nineteenth century.

Dozens of books have been written about the illustrated bird book, but original oil and watercolour pictures of birds have been largely neglected. *Great Bird Paintings of the World: The Old Masters* is the first in a series of volumes that will explore this fascinating subject.

Jan van Eyck
born Maaseik c.1390, died Bruges 1441

The Madonna with Canon George van der Paele
122 x 157 cm, dated 1436. Groeningemuseum, Bruges

Jan van Eyck and his elder brother Hubert, were among the earliest painters to use oil as a medium to bind their colour pigments. They used them with such wonderfully rich effects, that from their day, oil painting on wood and canvas has been the most popular medium with artists. The secret of their technique was the superimposition of successive layers of paint, exploiting their transparent qualities. They worked together on the remarkably beautiful Ghent altarpiece, an oil painting on five wooden panels called *The Adoration of the Lamb*, now in St Bavo Cathedral, until Hubert's early death in 1426, then Jan finished it alone.

The exact place in the Low Countries where Jan was born is not known but certain evidence of his activity as a painter occurs in 1422-24 when he was at The Hague court of John of Bavaria, the Count of Holland. After the Count's death on 5 January 1425, civil war broke out and Jan fled to Flanders, where he was taken into the service of the wealthy Philip III, Duke of Burgundy, at Bruges, both as a painter and *valet de chambre*.

The Duke greatly admired Jan's work, and respected him as a discreet servant. Jan was sent on several secret missions to European courts. One of these involved marriage negotiations for the Duke with the daughter of the King of Portugal when Jan's amazing ability to paint portraits that revealed the character of his sitter was of particular value to the Duke. Jan painted Isabella's portrait while in Portugal and took it back to Philip. The wedding took place with sumptuous festivities on 7 January 1430. Now, firmly in the Duke's favour and with an assured income, Jan bought a house at Bruges and lived there until his death.

Two years later, Jan van Eyck married Margaretha. When they had a son, the Duke was his godfather and gave Jan six silver cups. Jan continued to paint superb pictures, religious in subject but incorporating truthful portraits of all the people

in his paintings. He also achieved an astonishing degree of accuracy when depicting clothes, furnishings, and household objects in indoor scenes, or plants and animals in outdoor settings.

In 1436 he completed *The Madonna with Canon George van der Paele*, a work of his mature years, which included a portrait of the secular canon as revealing of his personality as of his person. By contrast, the portraits of the Madonna and Christ child, were stylized images. Christ is a beautiful baby with golden curls and intelligent, sad eyes, and Mary, though serene, lacks character traits.

Jan van Eyck's superb painting of the ring-necked parakeet is a marvellous piece of observation and realism. The subtle gradation of green tones, the red of eye and beak, and careful reflection of colour on the ring of the neck are beautifully and subtly painted. This is a surprising choice of bird in a religious painting of this period. Perhaps its rarity, even its appropriateness (green was the colour of love), appealed to him. The church had accorded the parrot a special status when it was observed that a parrot remained dry even in the heaviest downpour of rain because its feathers are so dense. For this reason, it became a symbol of virginal purity and so associated with the Virgin Mary.

The presence of this Afro-Asian species in the Low Countries at this time was worth recording. The bird may have been the property of the Duke or the canon.

Perhaps it had been a gift from the Portuguese at the time of the Duke's wedding, or brought back by Jan van Eyck himself from his visit to Portugal 1429-30. This was a decade or so after the Portuguese began to explore the islands west of Africa, but previously parrots were trans-shipped and imported into Europe overland from the east. Whatever its origin, this is one of the first members of the parrot family to have been painted in oils on wood.

Hieronymus Bosch

born s'Hertogenbosch c.1453, died s'Hertogenbosch 1516

The Garden of Earthly Delights

oil on wood panels, 220 x 195 cm (central panel), 220 x 97 cm (side panels)
Museo del Prado, Madrid

Bosch was a Netherlandish painter who was born, lived and died at s'Hertogenbosch, from which he might have got his name. *The Garden of Earthly Delights* may be regarded now as the high point of his painting career, but Bosch left other panels important in the art of his time because of their sense of mystery, visual inventiveness and religious sensitivity.

His painting is seen by us in terms of visual delights, but for him, and his fellow countrymen, many of the components of the painting had symbolic meaning, not least the animals taken from medieval bestiaries. Bosch was essentially a moralist, in spite of the sensual images in this painting.

Bosch's small home town was a triangular piece of land surrounded by water. The dominant building was a gothic cathedral, and much of Bosch's obsessive, haunted world is gothic in character. His teachers are unknown, the origin of his style uncertain, but his genius is shown in his ability to create an unsurpassed fantasy world of rare complexity disconcertingly juxtaposed to a normal, sane world. Whole books have been devoted to this single triptych, but we shall be excused, in the context of this book, if we view it both ornithologically, and as being very aptly named, for it is, as all gardens ought to be, full of delightful birds.

The Garden of Earthly Delights is spread across three wooden panels, the whole being a progress from the creation of mankind on the left, through a mad whirl of short-lived sensual pleasures regardless of spiritual welfare that takes up the large

central panel, to a vision of hell on the right hand panel. Birds, one is pleased to note, do not feature in the 'Hell' panel. The Garden of Eden panel includes half a dozen recognisable species, hooded crow, swans, ducks, egrets and a little owl, mixed in with some whimsical creatures with feathers sprouting in odd positions. The swirling flock of birds enjoying spiralling up through a tower punctuated with holes is amusing, especially the queue of birds at the bottom patiently awaiting their turn. However, it is the central panel, especially the cross-section enlarged here, that contains the greatest concentration of ornithological delights from the owl on the left being tenderly embraced by a man, across the panel to the owl on the right that no one in his right mind would dream of trying to embrace.

Some of the recognisable species in the centre are duck, hoopoe, woodpecker, robin, goldfinch, brambling, kingfisher, mallard, tawny owl, ibis, egret, great tit-mouse, black stork, jay, scops owl and spoonbills, all species with which Bosch would be familiar in his native Holland, and a peacock, no doubt seen in some wealthy merchant's ornamental garden.

Leonardo da Vinci
born Vinci 1452, died Cloux 1519

Leda
chalk, pen and ink and wash. Devonshire Collection, Chatsworth
Reproduced by permission of the Chatsworth Settlement Trustees

Cesare da Sesto
Italian 16th century

Leda and the Swan
Wilton House, Nr. Salisbury

Leonardo Vinci is considered to be among the greatest of the artists produced by the Renaissance because of his originality and his intellectual powers. The Italian Renaissance first developed in Tuscany and the city of Florence where Leonardo began his career as a painter. He was a Master in the Guild in 1472, while his earliest datable work is a drawing of a landscape of 1473 that shows he was already interested in the effect of heat and sunlight on rocks and other parts of a landscape. Also in the 1470s, he experimented with oil-painting techniques in order to achieve a subtle range of tonal values.

Whenever he tackled a new element, something as simple as drapery folds, or as complex as portraying the psychology of the disciples at the moment when Christ told them one of them was about to betray him in *The Last Supper*, Leonardo made many preliminary studies in order to arrive at perfection in detail and a unified composition.

Leonardo was an illegitimate son of a Florentine notary in whose home he was brought up. His restless intellect ranged over a wide variety of subjects, and any work he undertook was held up while he experimented with all the new ideas flooding into his mind. Consequently, he completed few of the paintings that he started. One of these few finished works is the *Mona Lisa* or *La Gioconda*, the celebrated portrait of the wife of a Florentine official painted between c.1500 and c.1504.

Leonardo's painted version of the legend of Leda and the swan was preceded by detailed drawings, many of which have survived, though his final panel painting has been lost. Leda, in Greek mythology, was the daughter of a King of Aetolia and the wife of a King of Sparta. She was loved by the supreme god Zeus, the bringer of light from heaven, for whom white was a sacred colour. He approached Leda in the form of a white, notably lecherous, swan. This theme has been used by numerous artists since Leonardo, and his own painting was copied by Raphael (a study c.1506-08, Royal Library, Windsor) and by Leonardo's main pupil, Cesare da Sesto. Cesare's copy is thought to be the one closest to Leonardo's original panel. The painting of the sinuous neck is typical of Leonardo's love of curving lines, and the wings of the swan (if a whooper swan, the wing

Leonardo's preparatory study for Leda and the Swan

18

Cesare da Sesto's painting of Leda and the Swan, *after Leonardo da Vinci*

span is 6ft.8ins.to 7ft. 9ins., 218 to 243cm) enfold Leda's body. The swan is placed on slightly higher ground to compensate for the difference in their height. Leda is holding a garland round the swan's neck and at her feet are many plants and flowers. Leonardo drew many flower studies throughout his life, introducing plants into the foregrounds of his paintings. At Windsor there are some exquisite pen and red chalk drawings of plants and flowers. In the foreground two pairs of twins emerge from egg shells. They are Castor and Pollux, Clytemnestra and Helen, the children of Leda, said to be by Zeus.

The elements of the picture celebrate the re-birth of nature in springtime. The Renaissance was so named to indicate a re-birth of Greek and Roman learning in the world of letters, and classical form in art and architecture. Leonardo was among the greatest creators of the High Renaissance in Italy.

Leonardo's study for a kneeling Leda cartoon, c.1506, was modified and the figure of Leda later changed to a standing figure, but the swan is substantially the same in the final panel painting. Cesare da Sesto's copy of Leonardo's 'Leda' (Wilton House) may have been painted in Leonardo's workshop.

Jacopo de' Barbari
born Venice c.1450, died Malines 1515/16

A Sparrowhawk
Oil on wood
Reproduced by courtesy of the Trustees, The National Gallery, London

Barbari is said to have been a Venetian painter, but he worked in Germany and the Netherlands from 1500 onwards. He and Dürer held one another in mutual respect, learning from one another like so many of the Italian and northern European artists who exchanged ideas during the exciting years of the Renaissance. In Germany, Barbari was regarded as a representative of the Italian Renaissance. He painted portraits and miniatures, and engraved on metal. In the course of his travels he met Dürer who acknowledged the debt he owed to Barbari for his knowledge of human anatomy. Barbari, in his turn, was influenced by Dürer, for example, in his two delicate and sensitively observed bird studies. Dürer referred to him as a 'charming painter' and though few of his works are known to us today, the two best known and most famous are both bird paintings of outstanding merit.

From 1500 he was a painter and illuminator to Emperor Maximilian (ruled 1493-1519), and Elector Friedrich III of Saxony, at the same time moving through other northern European courts, being employed by Philip of Burgundy, among others. He applied for a pension 1511-12 when he was described as being 'old and weak'. Since the two bird paintings are dated after 1500, they are work done in his mature years. The sparrowhawk is thought to be a fragment cut from a larger panel and as such is a modest little hunting trophy. The painting looks as though Barbari has used an illuminator's brush from the delicate touches for the tiny feathers and minute attention to every detail of the beak, strong legs, tail and long pointed wings. Sparrowhawks in profile are slender birds; in addition, this one is standing upright in order to look through the window. The strong sunlight that enters the simple enclosure creates deep shadows giving depth to the diagonal composition. He is wearing his falconry bell and is keenly alert, showing an interest in anything that moves in the world outside.

The exact date of the live sparrowhawk study is not known, but Barbari's painting of a dead partridge displayed against a wooden panel, with mailed gloves and a crossbow bolt, was painted in 1504. This is considered to be one of the first paintings, if not the earliest, of this genre, a still life of a bird in oil on wood. It was an innovation with far-reaching consequences, which has met with singular success in western painting ever since. Of all the species of bird that figure in still lifes, the partridge is by far the favourite, due to the beautifully marked pale blue, cream and buff feathering on the breast contrasting with the patch of dark red.

However superb the composition, brilliant the painting, sumptuous the colouring and breathtaking the skill and ingenuity that have combined to produce a masterpiece of still-life painting, all our current concern with conservation and preservation of wildlife biases most of us in favour of pictures of living birds. It is truly remarkable that Barbari should have left us not only a very early and magnificent painting of a dead partridge, but also a very early and splendid small panel of a single, live species of bird, the sparrowhawk.

Albrecht Dürer

born Nuremberg 1471, died Nuremberg 1528

Upper side of outstretched left wing of a young roller *Coracias garrulus*

water and body colour on vellum, heightened with white, 19.7 x 20.1cm
Graphische Sammlung Albertina, Vienna

Albrecht Dürer was the greatest painter of the German Renaissance. He lived in an age when religious painting dominated the art world in Northern Europe. Dürer was the son of a goldsmith who settled in Nuremberg in 1455. Albrecht was apprenticed first to his father, then bound to a painter for three years where he learned both to paint and execute woodcuts. This training as a medieval artisan came at a time when art was beginning to break free from craft guild restrictions, with their strict adherence to figures in pattern books that artists and craftsmen had referred to and reproduced in a mechanical fashion, for many years. Dürer, free of this restriction, looked at nature with fresh eyes and clear vision, then recorded the reality he saw with uncompromising fidelity.

The Dürer household always had many pets, and there is hardly a single important painting by Albrecht that did not include some animals. Even while still an apprentice in the 1480s, he produced a drawing of a *Lady Holding a Hawk*. Among his nature studies there is further evidence of his love of animals, when he sketched lobsters and crabs on the Adriatic coast, and lions, apes, camels, elks and bisons which reached Europe via Italian ports.

In the forests and fields surrounding his home at Nuremberg he came across squirrels, foxes, deer, hares, badgers and rabbits. On visits to the Tyrol he spotted ibexes and chamois high among the rocks. More remarkably, in 1515 he painted the first known picture of a rhinoceros. Many of these animals may be seen incorporated in his religious paintings. One of these, *The Virgin and Child With Animals,* a watercolour, 1505 (Albertina, Vienna) included dogs and sheep, but the number of bird species was more considerable. There were a woodpecker, stork, swans, two kinds of owl and, more improbably, a parakeet. A careful study of this same parakeet had been made in 1502-03 (Bibliotheca Ambrosiana, Milan), and Dürer was so pleased with such a rare specimen that he also painted it in a picture of *Adam and Eve* in 1504 (Pierpont Morgan Library, New York).

A bird easily seen in the gardens and woods of northern Europe was the yellow, green and black siskin, perched on the arm of the Christ child in a painting to which it gave its name, *Madonna with Siskin* 1506, (Berlin-Dahlem). Dürer also etched a remarkably good stork, then signed and dated it in 1517. A dead pochard became the subject of a still life (Museo Gulbenkian, Lisbon). He painted another single species still life, of a roller, signed and dated 1512. These are currently accepted as being genuine works by Dürer. Others, such as the *Little Owl,* are attributed. His monogram and a date were often added at a later date by another hand to copies of his work.

In 1512, he entered the service of Emperor Maximilian for whom he painted a series of miniature pictures of dozens of mammals and birds in the margins of a prayer book. The most spectacular, colourful and infinitely carefully observed study, however, was this wing of a roller, painted by Dürer in Nuremberg. The roller is one of the most colourful of European bird species. Rollers often perch prominently along the roadside on the look-out for large insects. They are very strong in flight when the contrasting dark and light colours of their wings are

shown off dramatically. In courtship display flight they roll and tumble, and even turn somersaults.

The roller's wing provided Dürer with the opportunity to study closely the wonderful range of colours on the feathers, also different characteristics of hard veins and stiffer barbs of the leading dark feathers by contrast with the softer, downy inner feathers. Using superb brushwork, Dürer recorded the structure and shape of this wing as a true record of the beauty of nature. However, he had another purpose in mind. Close scrutiny of angels in religious paintings of this period, including Dürer's own religious pictures, show that the angels were equipped with birds' wings for flight.

An angel with birds' wings, painted by Caravaggio. Note also the pebbles at the feet of the angel. These reappear in Caravaggio's Still Life of Birds, *p.43.*

Hans Burgkmair
born Augsburg 1473, died Augsburg 1531

St John at Patmos
pine panel, 153 x 135 cm, signed and dated 1518
Alte Pinakothek, Munich

Hans Burgkmair was born in Augsburg, the son of a painter who gave him his early training. His career followed the traditional pattern of a training by local masters, followed by a period away travelling in Germany and the Netherlands, returning home where he became a member of the guild, marriage, and setting up his own studio in Augsburg. Two things then occurred that took this talented artist out of the ordinary, into the circle of extraordinary artists. First, at the Augsburg Diet in 1500, he met Emperor Maximilian who became his most important employer and patron. The following year Burgkmair created the first coloured woodcut using colour blocks, one of his jobs being to make woodcut illustrations for Maximilian. Secondly, in 1507, he travelled to Italy for a short visit, following which he became the most important artist of the Augsburg school to bring Italian influences into southern German painting. In this, he played a similar role to that of Dürer in Nuremberg in northern Germany.

In 1516, the Emperor granted him a coat of arms as a mark of special recognition. Ten years later, Burgkmair took the precaution to buy a pension from Augsburg town as security for himself and his wife in their old age. He died at Augsburg in 1531.

Burgkmair's painting of St John the Evangelist at Patmos (an island between Italy and Greece) was recorded as being in the private gallery of Emperor Maximilian. It is the central panel of a triptych altarpiece, signed and dated 1518. This painting is a delightful example of conformity and individuality. Burgkmair conformed to the strict discipline exercised by the church which forced artists to paint religious subjects almost exclusively. However, though St John receiving divine revelation while writing the last book in the Bible (The Revelation of St John the Divine) is the central theme, Burgkmair has surrounded St John with some beautifully painted examples of the natural world. What is most remarkable is the sumptuous landscape of luxurious flowers, shrubs and fruit-bearing trees, and the sheer number of animals, reptiles, even shells, that are all in correct proportion one to another.

The painting is now in the Munich Alte Pinakothek, in a slightly enlarged form. Early in the seventeenth century additions were made to the top and sides of this central panel, enabling another artist to add five or six more bird species. The birds in the painting can be identified as woodpecker, goldfinch, blue titmouse, kingfisher, redstart, green macaw, great titmouse, wagtail and an eagle. Many saints acquired a bird icon that immediately identified the saint in stained glass windows, statues and paintings. St John the Evangelist's bird was an eagle, the bird in this painting nearest to him.

Hans Holbein

born Augsburg 1497/8, died London 1543

Portrait of the Falconer Robert Cheseman Carrying a Hooded Falcon

oil on wood, 59 x 62.5cm, dated 1533, Mauritshuis, The Hague

Holbein painted the portrait of Henry VIII which immediately springs to mind whenever that monarch's name is mentioned. He painted other remarkable portraits that are as revealing of their sitter's personality and something of the age in which they lived. There is an immediacy, a sense of dignity and qualities of stillness and precision in every detail of dress and surroundings that mark Holbein as a wonderful artist and outstanding portraitist.

Hans Holbein was born in Augsburg, the son of a painter. He first worked in Basle and Lucerne from 1515 to 1526, then spent two years in London before returning to Basle. Due to the violent disturbances of the Reformation, Holbein decided to settle in England where he believed the arts and scholarship were flourishing under Henry VIII's encouragement. It was while he was in England that he painted three remarkable portraits that included equally memorable birds.

Holbein's superb portrait of a *Lady With a Squirrel and a Starling*, which caused such interest when it was purchased for the National Gallery, London, in 1992, recorded Sir Thomas More's daughter with her pets. The red squirrel is characteristically poised, chewing on a nut that it holds in its paws, and with a glint in its eye that suggests it was not always a perfectly behaved pet. The starling is also caught in a typical pose, restlessly alert, though its grasp on a thin twig is distinctly unreal.

There is nothing wrong with the firm seating on the falconer's glove of this lanner falcon, one of two paintings of portraits including falcons in The Mauritshuis, The Hague. A falconer must remain calmly in control at all times when handling and flying his birds. Robert Cheseman is monumentally calm, and gently reassures

the hooded bird by a slight touch on its breast feathers. Robert Cheseman (1485-1547) lived at Dormanswell, Norwood, Middlesex, and had been cofferer and keeper of the wardrobe to Henry VII.

Both man and bird are projected forward by the very plain background, broken only by the gold lettering that Holbein frequently used in later years. The elegant form of the magnificent falcon has a three-dimensional quality. The latent power and weight of the bird are conveyed even though the wings are relaxed. The feather markings and colouring, with the light falling across the back, are painted with a draughtsman's accurate recording of detail combined with a painter's eye for composition, chiaroscuro (effects of light and shade) and perspective.

Falconry was a popular sport in England from the ninth century and was practised by successive kings and noblemen. Birds were imported from the East and Europe. The birds were carefully graded according to their powers of flight and ability to fly

down different quarry, and equated with a descending order in the nobility. Emperors were assigned eagles, vultures and merlins, kings had gyrfalcons, and so on, down through dukes, earls, barons and knights to esquires who were allowed a lanner (which was regarded as being easy to train to take partridge early in the season), ladies a merlin, to priests who could fly a sparrowhawk and a servant the kestrel. Being familiar with all the falconry terms and etiquette was the mark of an educated man. The Tudors were keen falconers, especially Henry VIII and his daughter Elizabeth. The art of hunting with trained birds of prey only declined in the late seventeenth century when sporting firearms were improved.

Holbein died during the terrible plague epidemic in London in 1543 when at the height of his powers and fame.

Ludger tom Ring

born Munster 1522, died Brunswick 1584

A Great Bustard Cock and Other Birds

oil on panel, 61 x 40.6 cm, Christie's, London

Ludger tom Ring the Younger was the son of Ludger tom Ring (1496-1547) in whose studio he received his early training. He travelled in the Netherlands, then worked at Munster until about 1550, during which time his father died. Ring was obliged to leave Munster, perhaps because he was a Protestant, and so he went to England. By 1569 he was able to return to Brunswick which became his home for the rest of his life. He obtained citizenship there, and married Ilse Bardenwerper, the daughter of a distinguished family.

Ring was a portrait and still life artist. He painted some exquisite studies of flowers in oils on paper and used them, with some dead birds and a live African grey parrot, cockerel and dove, in the first kitchen piece in German still life painting, *The Marriage at Cana* (the marriage feast is in the background). The vase and basket of flowers in this domestic kitchen scene were novel, and so was Ring's painting of *A Great Bustard Cock and Other Birds*.

This picture of the great bustard is surrounded by carefully spaced, equally faithfully painted brambling, juvenile tree sparrow, faded robin, adult tree sparrow and a pair of blackbirds. All the work done here clearly shows the painter's love for the beauty and form of birds. The delicate shading, colouration and markings of the plumage of the male bustard admirably convey its form. There is also very careful attention to detail in the beak, eye and scaly skin of legs and feet. While the remaining birds might have been neatly placed, they have been shown in poses that display their characteristic features in a charming and subtle manner. The male brambling, top left, is in winter plumage with very strong pattern markings down the back. The tree sparrow is shown from the side so that its black cheek patch and white neck ring, by which it is clearly distinguished from the more common house sparrow, are visible. The tree sparrow is very localised in Britain. The male blackbird is entirely black but the female is dark brown with a slightly paler brown throat and breast, which she is showing off by raising her wings. He is one of the finest song birds, often the first to start singing in the morning.

The great bustard is a glamorous bird, even though the male is Europe's heaviest bird. He is twice as big as the female and weighs 18 kilogrammes. His glamour is derived from long throat whiskers that decorate his lavender-grey neck in the breeding season, and a brown-red breast band that develops as he grows older. This is an extremely shy bird and very dignified, until the mating season when a transformation takes place in the male whenever a female shows the slightest interest in him. He then appears to dissolve into a huge bundle of shimmering white feathers atop strutting greenish legs. This wonderful bird used to roam the Russian and Siberian steppes in huge flocks and was found across Europe westwards into England. It is so popular as a savoury game bird, however, that it now only survives in small areas in Ring's native Germany, parts of Spain and in eastern Europe.

Ludger tom Ring's painting of this bird was not so much a commemoration of a rarity, but a record of a very remarkable species. It is neither purely a draughtsman's study nor a true conventional still life picture, but a stage somewhere between the two. Nonetheless, it was sold in London in 1988 for £120,000, a clear indication of its quality.

Georg Flegel

born Olmütz 1566, died Frankfurt am Main 1638

Still Life of Birds

oil on canvas, 52.5 x 54.5 cm, signed and dated 1637

Flegel is another German artist who took great pleasure in painting everyday objects with such loving care and observation as to make each an item of beauty, either derived from its shape, texture or colour, sometimes a combination of these elements. His fellow countrymen, Dürer and Burgkmair, had each contributed to the development of painting still life objects, but Flegel went a stage further. They had painted the objects as part of the scenery in their major works. We have looked at their careful preparatory studies, and seen the manner in which they skilfully included birds in their religious paintings. Ludger tom Ring occupied an intermediary place by assembling a number of still life studies into a neat arrangement. Flegel brought together these unconnected elements in order to create a new and different kind of still life picture.

Still life is the English term, translated from the Dutch *Stilleven*, meaning the class of pictures representing inanimate objects. The French term, *nature morte*, conveys the same meaning. The term is appropriate for household objects, less so for flowers and fruit, and acceptable for dead game. However, live birds, insects and small mammals are often included in still life paintings, when a better term should be found for such paintings. From the very earliest still life paintings, live birds were included, a particular favourite being a brightly coloured parrot.

Flegel learned his art while working as an apprentice in the studio of a Flemish painter, Lucan van Valckenborch. In 1597 he acquired citizen's rights in Frankfurt and stayed there until he died. He specialized in banquet scenes, breakfast and flower still lifes, so that he is regarded now as being the most important representative of early German still life painters.

The choice of objects, while appearing random, is far from being so. In his *Dessert Still Life* and *Large Display Meal*, Flegel's contemporaries would have known not only why each different object was present, but would have been able to read the meaning of those objects. A green parrot represented 'good', a mouse 'evil', a parrot and butterfly 'the resurrection' (both emerge from an egg), and so on. The extraordinary complexity of religious symbolism that is present in our Flegel picture (e.g. the parrot guarding the bowl of fruit or nuts, representing spiritual principles being guarded), would have given his contemporaries added pleasure in reading the message in the painting. We enjoy it simply as a charming picture of well-painted natural history subjects, where every bird is meticulously spaced and positioned to show each to its best plumage advantage.

This is our first oil painting on canvas, for Flegel envisaged it as a small, self-contained picture.

The dead birds are a woodcock and a partridge. There are, in addition, eight living bird species and several other small creatures with the fruits and seeds. In the foreground there are a hawfinch and chaffinch, while the centre of the picture is occupied by a lapwing and a dove. Perched among the branches of the tree are four colourful birds, a waxwing, a kingfisher and a blue titmouse. The parrot, a blue-fronted amazon, is very similar to that in other Flegel paintings, shown in the same pose, performing the same protective duty.

Georg Flegel

Still Life with Red-faced Lovebird

water coloured drawing, 23.4 x 17.9cm, Staatlichen Museen, Berlin

Flegel has painted this picture in watercolours, with the red-faced lovebird as an important feature in the composition. He painted the same bird, in oils on wood, in a *Dessert Still Life* (Alte Pinakothek, Munich) where the bird is perched on the edge of a porcelain bowl containing nuts. He is using a male bird of this species, which had green plumage, more yellowish on the underparts, and the distinguishing forehead and facial area of orange-red. The bill is coral red and the iris dark brown and legs grey. Flegel has not been able to show the bright blue rump nor the green lateral tail feathers edged with bright red and yellow and subterminally barred with black. This species of parrot frequents areas of central and central-western Africa where they feed on seeds, fruits, berries and leaf buds and can be troublesome in crop-growing districts where they eat both the green and ripening grain. They spend a lot of time on or near the ground, feeding on grass seeds. They also sleep hanging upside-down.

Flegel has painted a very real and life-like red-faced lovebird, house fly, fruit and nuts. He has also painted a picture that shows the forces of good (parrot) and evil (flies were creatures of the devil) fighting for the soul of man. The human soul is represented by the fruit – the strawberries and cherries which were considered to be the fruits of paradise. Parrots were also elements of the resurrection, so the disease and corruption that the evil fly will inflict on the fruit will be overcome. Nuts were also symbolic, walnuts, according to St Augustine, being symbols of Christ. Here we have hazelnuts and almonds which, with the fruit, were served as desserts as a conclusion to a banquet of between six to eight courses in aristrocratic households of the period. So this painting has yet another significance. It is a social record of the new luxury items of the time, the exotic pet bird and the rare, expensive food.

At this early phase of the still life genre, it was usual to arrange a bowl or basket in isolation and concentrate attention on the contents which were arranged, for the most part, so that they did not overlap. Flegel has been careful to paint the shadows cast by the different objects lying in the path of a light source from the bottom left of the picture. The picture is not painted at eye level, but we are looking slightly up toward it. Flegel's *Still Life with a Red-faced Lovebird* is a deceptively simple watercolour of great immediate charm and hidden meaning.

Jan Brueghel

born Brussels 1568, died Antwerp 1625

Noah's Ark
oil on canvas
The Walters Art Gallery, Baltimore, Maryland

Jan Brueghel was a member of the most famous family of Dutch painters in the sixteenth/seventeenth centuries. Jan's father, Pieter Brueghel (1525/30-1569), was the greatest Dutch artist of the sixteenth century because he was so innovative, as well as being a superb painter. Pieter's last picture, called *Magpie on the Gallows* 1568 (Darmstadt, Hessisches Landesmuseum), has a luminous, panoramic landscape with groups of small figures (the magpie being a tiny bird on the gibbet). His son, Jan, had a similar ability to create large landscapes of great beauty, but his small groups of figures were animals, rather than people. Jan inherited other ideas from his father. Pieter had not taken his subjects from the classical world, from history or mythology, but painted the world as he found it and treated biblical subjects as though contemporary events. Jan inherited this independent attitude, which is demonstrated in his version of the story of *Noah's Ark*. Jan's own son, another Jan (1601-1678) known as Jan the Younger to avoid confusion with his father Jan the Elder, painted very similar subjects to those of his father. Jan the Younger inherited his father's workshop and imitated his style (see *Allegory of Air*, page 40).

Jan Brueghel the Elder's early pictures of shells, insects, flowers and birds were small, and frequently done in oils on copper. Acquaintances called him 'Brueghel de Vlours' for his skill in painting flowers (often 'vlours' is wrongly translated as

1. Swan   2. Heron   3. Purple gallinule   4. Long-eared owl   5. Pheasant   6. Scarlet macaw
7. Blue and gold macaw   8. Bird of paradise   9. Ostrich   10. Turkey   11. Pigeons   12. Duck

Bats, here improbably shown flying in broad daylight, were classified as birds at this date. Linnaeus correctly classified bats as mammals in 1758. With the exception of birds, bats are the only surviving animals that possess the organs of true flight.

velours or velvet). Later, he painted larger pictures, on canvas, that were brilliant in colour, spirited, and realistically executed. When his reputation grew, he was in demand either to paint landscapes or add animals, flowers and other ornamental elements for other eminent painters, including Rubens.

He travelled repeatedly between Brussels and Antwerp in order to visit the royal menagerie with its aviaries and gardens at Het Park near Coudenberg, belonging to Archduke Albert and Isabella. The Counts of Louvain (and later the Dukes of Brabant) had settled on the higher ground in the south east of the city, at Coudenberg, Brussels where a castle for the dukes was completed in 1047. Brueghel went to Coudenberg to paint Isabella in Het Park, feeding deer and surrounded by peacocks, cranes, muscovy and shelducks, mallard, a bustard, barnacle goose, moorhen and heron among other birds. This picture now hangs in Rubens' House in Antwerp.

Brueghel painted many forest scenes, probably based on memories of the woods at Het Park, and used these as backgrounds for his pictures of *The Garden of Eden*, *Earthly Paradise*, and *Orpheus Charming the Animals*, which he painted repeatedly. These subjects provided artists who were nature lovers with the perfect excuse to fill their canvases with mammals and birds, reptiles, trees and flowers.

Brueghel's *Noah's Ark* is a remarkable, early canvas representing this subject. However, the real subject here is the animal kingdom, with the ark relegated to the distant background. The animal species in this picture are probably indicative of those present in the menagerie. They are paired, ready to go into the ark. The camels are being prodded in the right direction by a man in Flemish late sixteenth century dress, but the rest of the animals appear reluctant to leave the beautiful park. Most of the birds are sitting in the tree on the left, but on the right hand side a pair of bats (then thought to be in the same scientific group as birds) fly near two birds of paradise. The first birds of paradise had been brought to Spain in 1522, already skinned and with the feet removed by the native Aru Island collectors so that Europeans thought they had no legs and feet and lived constantly on the wing. They were so beautiful, that Spaniards decided they must have come from paradise, hence their name. The birds on or by the stream are swans, ducks, egrets and herons.

The turkeys, placed so prominently in the foreground, were a species introduced by the Spaniards from Central America between 1525 and 1530. They had been taken to England by John Cabot's ship-mate William Strickland from the St Lawrence region in 1497/8. By 1541 they had bred so successfully in England that Archbishop Thomas Cranmer forbade his clergy to serve more than one turkey at a banquet. By 1600, they were Christmas fare in most households. Although now familiar, they still had great visual appeal to artists.

In this ideal animal world that Brueghel has painted, the ring-tailed cat climbing the tree where so many birds are perched is not causing the least alarm. The mischievous dog, barking at the gallinule, provokes only a mild stare of disapproval. Among the exotic species, a pair of ostriches regard the scene with interest, and two pairs of macaws, blue and gold with red, form decorative high points on the top left. Getting all these contented animals into the ark is going to be a lengthy business.

Jan Brueghel

The Garden of Eden
oil on canvas. Courtesy of the Trustees of the V & A.

The first bird of paradise skins arrived in Seville on 6 September 1522 on Ferdinand Magellan's ship Victoria. *The natives had removed the bones and legs from the five specimens, which gave rise to the myth that these birds were* Paradisaea apoda – *legless, as Linnaeus named them in 1758.*

Jan's father died when he was one year old, so he was brought up by his grandmother, Marie de Bessemers, who gave him his first lessons in painting. Like Pieter before him, he was given the opportunity to travel to Italy and visited Naples in 1590, Rome the following year and worked under the protection of Cardinal Borromeo in Milan before returning to Antwerp in 1596. He was such a successful painter of landscape, becoming the greatest painter of his day of the woodland scene, in particular, that his work was sought after both in the Netherlands and Italy. The Italian influence on his work may be seen in the warm sunlight in his skies and where it casts golden tints across the landscape.

The Garden of Eden has many similarities to *Noah's Ark*, but the human figures are even smaller and the animals are brought forward so that the viewer feels a part of this peaceful scene. The luxuriance of fruit and flowers could only be the work of an artist exceptionally skilled in painting them, and each animal has been caught in characteristic pose. By closing the foliage overhead and making it so much denser, Brueghel suggests the garden rather than a woodland glade. His landscape across the river is expansive, suggesting the whole world is out there, waiting to be explored.

There are some different birds in this scene. A bustard is standing just within the picture on the left. In the tree, an African grey parrot is peering down, perched with some owls, macaws, toco toucans from Brazil and The Guianas, and many small foreign and European birds. Quite extraordinarily, Brueghel has painted a beautiful small study of a bird of paradise that is perched and has quite long legs, neatly exploding the myth that these birds are legless. In 1824 René Lesson, a

French ship's apothecary, discovered a live bird on New Guinea and finally established the truth about this bird's anatomy.

The most surprising bird in this picture is a penguin, which was perhaps so newly arrived in a menagerie that Brueghel could not quite believe his eyes, nor its anatomy, for he has given it haunches, like a dog. The Dutch discovered the Magellanic penguin in the Straits of Magellan in 1599. The jackass penguin, that occurs off the coast of South Africa, was also known in Europe. Both are the same length, and it is not possible to be certain, from this rear view, which is pictured here.

Jan Brueghel
The Element of Air

oil on copper, 21.2 x 31.7 cm
Sotheby's, London

Jan Brueghel the Elder painted two series of allegorical subjects, one set based on the five senses (touch, taste, smell, sound and sight) and another on the four elements, air, fire, earth and water. These titles gave artists almost limitless opportunities for genre and still life scenes decorated with an exuberant and imaginative collection of objects. His son, Jan the Younger (1601-1678) painted similar series, very close in style and content to those of his father. The son's rendering of *The Four Elements,* oil on copper (47.7 x 77.5 cm) may be seen at Kingston Lacy, Wimborne Minster, Dorset. Another complete set of four *Elements*, by the father, is preserved in Rome in the Galleria Doria Pamphilij. These are larger oils, painted on panels 55 x 93 cm. Common to all these versions are human figures painted by an artist friend of the Brueghel family, Hendrick van Balen (1575-1632).

The Greek philosopher Empedocles, born in the fifth century before Christ, was interested in biology, medicine and physics. He discovered that air is a substance, distinct from empty space. He went further, and proposed the theory that air, with fire, water, and earth were the four elements from which all substances were composed. Today, we still speak of fish being in their natural element, meaning water and birds in theirs, meaning air.

Artists could use the painting of *Air* to include every known bird species, though fewer birds could be incorporated legitimately in a picture of *Water*. *Earth* and *Fire* do not lend themselves as appropriate settings for birds. Two paintings, oil on copper, of *The Element of Air* and *The Element of Water* from a set of four, were sold at Sotheby's, London in July 1993. They were signed and dated 'BRVEGHEL 1611'. *Air*, reproduced here (see also page 6), has a wonderful feeling of movement, with a rainbow and shafts of lightning in a dramatic sky where a gap in the clouds reveals Apollo, the sun god, driving a chariot and horses to bring in the new day. This is one of the most remarkably vivid blue skies with sunlight painted in this period.

Although many of the birds are small and the pairs are not always close together, it is possible to identify over forty species. There are four different owls, long-eared next to barn, a little and a tawny owl. The birds of paradise, with long tail

streamers, appear to be flying at great speed, and, as usual, are placed very high in the sky. Brueghel once again paints bats among the birds, close by the birds of paradise.

The number of birds on the wing, and, even more remarkable, the number with their legs correctly aligned along their bodies, is a truly impressive ornithological feat at this period. In the top right hand corner, some birds of prey are hunting and the heron is under attack. Perhaps it would not be too fanciful to suggest that Brueghel has attempted to paint the 'jizz' of several birds, centuries before that word was invented or the plumage patterns of birds in flight were included in field guides. Brueghel has painted some birds as seen from underneath, but the colouring of the bird and its tail and wings make identification possible.

The treecreeper is correctly positioned on the underside of the tree trunk, working its way up, searching for insects among the lichen. The head of the dodo antedates Savery's picture of the dodo by several years. The sea birds, perhaps black-headed gulls in winter plumage, are unusual in seventeenth century paintings where few are represented.

The goddess carrying a celestial globe in her right hand and a handful of feathers from the ostrich and peacock (perhaps also the flamingo and eagle) may be Artemis, the daughter of Zeus and sister of Apollo. As goddess of the moon, she would take her departure as the sun rose. She was also a goddess of wild life and all young creatures.

Caravaggio

born Caravaggio, Lombardy 1571, died Porto Ercole 1610

Still Life of Birds
oil on canvas, 103.5 x 173 cm. Galleria Borghese, Rome

Caravaggio's personal name was Michelangelo Meris or Amerighi, but he is known by his place of birth, Caravaggio, a town near Milan. Before leaving Lombardy to go to Rome, he spent several years as an apprentice in Milan. Caravaggio said that he could find quite enough teachers in nature, without going to other artists for tuition. He became part of the trend established by earlier Italian painters of the sixteenth century, to 'return to nature'. He, too, found inspiration and an endless source of stimulation in the study of ordinary people and everyday objects, besides natural history subjects.

His life was extraordinarily tempestuous. When he reached Rome, where he hoped to make his fortune, he started on a course that led to quarrels, adventures, flight, imprisonment for manslaughter and every kind of trouble imaginable, stemming mainly from his violent temper. Throughout it all, he produced one masterpiece after another. These are characterized by deep inner strength and poetic understanding, undisturbed by outside events, that are the hallmarks of the truly great master painters.

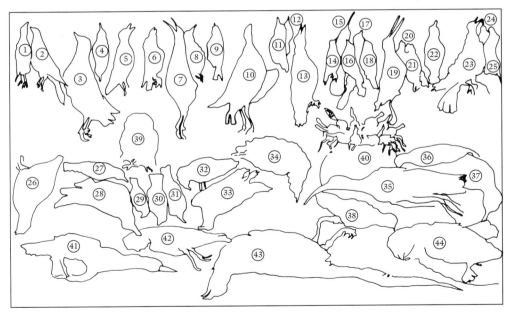

1. Quail   2. Turtle dove   3. Woodcock   4. Lesser spotted woodpecker   5. Starling   6. Hawfinch
7. Water rail   8. Calandra lark   9. Greenfinch   10. Lapwing   11. Kingfisher   12. Wren
13. Green woodpecker   14. Goldfinch   15. Bee-eater?   16. Chaffinch   17. Great grey shrike
18. Robin   19. Snipe   20. ?   21. Bullfinch   22. Wryneck   23. Cuckoo   24. ?   25. Cirl bunting
26. Rock partridge   27. Golden oriole   28. Teal   29. Great titmouse   30. Thrush
31. Blackbird   32. Great spotted woodpecker   33. Wood pigeon   34. Partridge   35. Curlew
36. Stock dove   37. Smew   38. Plover?   39. Little owl   40. Plucked wheatears on dish on basket   41. Mallard   42. Jay   43. Pheasant   44. Barn owl.

Today, we use the term 'Caravaggesque' to denote naturalistic depiction of objects, lighting from outside the picture, and the expressive use of light and shade, for these were his techniques. In these areas, Caravaggio influenced seventeenth century painters, notably Velazquez and Rembrandt, also Rubens who saw his work in Rome and was a profound admirer.

Caravaggio's bird picture *Still Life of Birds* was painted at the beginning of his career, with one or two other notable still life pictures. The innovation, in this particular composition, was the treatment of the birds with the same intense seriousness, giving importance and dramatic force to each, as was formerly reserved for objects in religious paintings. The birds are painted entirely for their own beauty of colour and form, and not merely as additional decorative parts of a larger scene. In addition, he gave the birds a tangible reality. Each one is hanging there and a great gust of wind would surely ruffle their feathers.

The array of some forty different birds is grouped around the compelling image of a live, inscrutably knowing little owl. Most of the birds are so skilfully recorded that an ornithologist can readily identify them, only two or three being half hidden or so much in shadow as to render them difficult to see.

We are used to seeing birds in the field either from the side or dorsally, and artists usually paint living birds from those views and, traditionally, at eye level. Most still life painters, however, portray dead birds ventrally, upside down and with wings splayed to reveal the underside. This painting by Caravaggio is extraordinary in the varied positioning of the life-size birds. Another unusual feature is the number of bird species, all to be found in the Italian countryside.

Daniel Fröschl

born Augsburg 1573, died Prague 1613

Two Woodpeckers

watercolour and body colour on paper, heightened with white, 19.5 x 25.5cm.
signed, dated 1589, and inscribed in pen and brown ink
Österreichische National Bibliothek, Vienna

Daniel was the son of a graduate lawyer, Hieronymus Fröschl of Augsburg. He went to Florence and worked there for the Grand Duke of Tuscany from about 1597-1603. While he was employed there he also obtained the patronage of Emperor Rudolph II, on 28 December 1601, as a miniaturist, paid fifteen florins a month.

Rudolph's father was Maximilian II (ruled 1564-76), a Holy Roman Emperor with his court at Vienna. He had established a menagerie at Ebersdorf near Vienna, where he housed leopards, an elephant and a free-flying pet pelican. His son also became an enthusiast for natural science and kept exotic animals, including the first Australian cassowary to be seen in Europe. It was brought by the Dutch to be exhibited at Amsterdam, then it was bought by the Elector of Cologne and given as a present to Rudolph. The Emperor also acquired a connoisseur's passion for art. The two interests combined to make Rudolph a keen collector. He was highly appreciative of Dürer's art and purchased some of his watercolours. Dürer's painting of the wing of the roller is known to have been in Rudolph's Imperial Treasure Chamber.

In 1583 Rudolph moved his court from Vienna to Prague, and there Fröschl went to take up his post of miniaturist, just one among a whole galaxy of artists, scientists and litterati who flocked from all over Europe to enjoy the Emperor's patronage and, incidentally, his art collection. For Fröschl there was a special role to play in this exciting time of purchasing works of art, for besides his job as court painter, on 1 May 1607 he was appointed as Rudolph's antiquary and curator. This task left him little opportunity to paint, for he spent most of his time compiling an inventory of the Emperor's art collection. When Rudolph died in 1612, Fröschl unfortunately, was accused of misappropriating objects from the treasure chamber. Fröschl died in Prague on 15 October 1613.

It will be immediately obvious that Fröschl's pen and ink drawing with watercolours heightened with white of the two woodpeckers has affinities with Dürer's wing of a roller. There is the same concern to paint the softness of the plumage, the tiny straying down feathers where they peep out from under the main feathers, and attention to the varying intensity of colour. This, too, is fine watercolour painting.

The inscription appears to be clear and informative, but it poses some problems. The words 'Alsterspecht od(er) Baumheckel' are alternative German names for woodpecker. There are two species of woodpecker in this painting. The dead bird at the top is a great spotted woodpecker, *Dendrocopos major*, a species with which British ornithologists are familiar, and the live bird is the middle spotted woodpecker, *Dendrocopos medius*, a resident of continental Europe.

Although the inscription has two styles of handwriting, it seems likely that the artist wrote the third line on a separate occasion. Authenticity is not doubted, since there are other watercolours of birds by Fröschl similarly signed. The date, however, 1 November 1589, infers that Daniel was possessed of precocious talent to be able to produce work of such meticulous observation and artistic quality at the age of sixteen. His subsequent work confirms this.

Dürer's and Fröschl's watercolour studies were intended to be meticulously accurate records of the species. They worked with watercolours and body colour, and these paintings on paper were placed in albums. They were kept away from the light to prevent fading. Fröschl's watercolours of birds were almost certainly done specifically at the Emperor's command. When recording many species, speed was essential. Working in watercolours was quicker than using oil paints that take some time to dry between applications of the different layers of paint. The choice of watercolours was made for speed, ability to reproduce an accurate rendering of the subject, and the wish of the patron. If the patron had wanted a painting to hang on the wall, he would have required an oil painting. The different media were used for different purposes, each recognised for its own potential, from the very beginnings of bird art, using panels and canvas or paper, oil paints or watercolours.

Peter Paul Rubens

born Siegen 1577, died Antwerp 1640

Ganymede and the Eagle

oil on canvas, 203 x 203 cm, c.1611-12
With the kind permission of HSH the Prince of Schwarzenberg

Rubens was a many-sided genius. He was among the greatest European painters of any age, an antiquarian and scholar, a skilful diplomat, monarchist and, as a devout Catholic, a patriot of the Spanish Netherlands. He won the respect of Philip IV of Spain and Charles I of England so that a peace treaty between them was secured. Charles I knighted him for his diplomatic achievements in 1629 and he was also ennobled by the King of Spain.

In 1598, after his apprenticeship, he was made a member of the Painters' Guild in Antwerp. He went to Italy two years later and became court painter to the Duke of Mantua. In 1603 the Duke sent him to Rome to copy some pictures and then on a mission to Philip III of Spain. The illness and death of his mother took him back to Antwerp in 1608. He quickly found two powerful patrons there, married in 1609 and built a house with a studio two years later. He was a very disciplined and methodical worker, rising at four every morning. Following mass, he worked until five in the afternoon, and then went riding. After the death of his first wife, he married the beautiful sixteen-year old Hélène Fourment, with whom he was extremely happy. He often painted her, sometimes accompanied by their children.

Soon after Rubens' return from Italy, he became the leading figure of the Antwerp school, influencing younger painters such as Van Dyck, Jordaens and Snyders, who were either his pupils or collaborated with him in paintings. Rubens' output was enormous. Any difficulties in compiling a complete catalogue of his work, due to the number of items, is compounded by his pupils, collaborators and colleagues working so closely in his style that it is not always possible to distinguish between them.

Both during and after his stay in Italy, he aimed at equalling the great masters by tackling subjects on a monumental scale. For his figures, Rubens created an ideal human type – men of heroic aspect and sensual women. He used warm, rich colours with golden tones. His delineation was pictorial, without clearcut lines but integrated into the light surrounding it.

Rubens was attracted to mythological subjects by their drama and the opportunity they gave to work on a grand scale. The rape of Ganymede was just such a story. The young Ganymede was carried off by the eagle of Zeus, on account of his beauty, to be cup-bearer to the gods in Olympus. Eternal life and youth were granted after drinking the nectar in the golden cup of Hebe. In the painting, Ganymede is taking the cup before becoming cup-bearer at the feast of gods taking place in the top left corner of the picture.

Rubens' youth is classically idealized and rather large to be lifted by an eagle. He seems to be participating in events quite contentedly while supported by the wing of the eagle. It is a wonderfully naturalistic eagle whose physical presence and the precision of painting in every part of its feathers suggest that Rubens surely had made close observation of a living bird. It was painted c.1611-12 and Rubens may have found an eagle in the menagerie of the Hapsburg family and sketched it earlier. The pose of the eagle, feet apart and wings outspread, reminds one of the

heraldic device of the Hapsburgs. Rubens was quite capable of painting wild beasts and birds, as the virtuosity of this eagle demonstrates, but he asked Snyders to paint the eagle in his other picture with this bird as a central motif (*Prometheus Bound*).

Early civilisations were almost unanimous in regarding the eagle as a symbol of the divine, in this instance the symbol of the Greeks' supreme god, Zeus (or Roman equivalent, Jupiter). As Zeus' bird it was also the bearer of the thunderbolt and lightning. The eagle was chosen for its characteristics of swift and high flight, training of its young, keen eyesight, nesting in inaccessible places, and its longevity and strength. Rembrandt (page 48) has painted an eagle of awesome, god-like power, the bird of the thunderbolt and lightning. Rubens chose to portray it as a servant of the god, using its strength to intervene in the affairs of man.

Rembrandt Harmenszoon van Rijn

born Leiden 1606, died Amsterdam 1669

The Rape of Ganymede

oil on canvas, 177 x 129 cm, signed and dated 'Rembrandt ft 1635'
Staatliche Kunstsammlungen, Dresden

Rembrandt was born in Leiden, the son of a miller. He attended the university for about a year and then became apprenticed to an obscure painter for three years. During a short period in Amsterdam he learned to paint historical pictures and became acquainted with the work of Caravaggio and early Baroque artists. He returned to Leiden to paint, from 1625 to 1631/2 when he established himself in Amsterdam and became a successful portrait painter. His output was prodigious and there are about 650 paintings by him of which some sixty are self-portraits, among these an unusual picture of the artist holding up a dead bittern, (Dresden Gallery, 1639). Rembrandt painted other birds, for he made many still life studies. He painted a girl with two dead peacocks of wonderful colouring and lighting. *A Knight with a Falcon* is in the Gothenburg Art Gallery. He painted birds with remarkably free brushwork to create the depth and softness of feathers. His still life paintings have only one or two animals as motifs and he complements this with strongly focused lighting. His work is amazing for its technical virtuosity, psychological expression, and realism.

Rembrandt painted his version of *The Rape of Ganymede* fifteen years after Rubens' picture was completed. It is in the Dresden Gallery which also has a pen and wash drawing showing how Rembrandt tackled the compositional problems for this subject. He drew the eagle taking a reluctant child (rather than a youth) with his parents, the King Tros and Queen Callirrhoë of Troy, vainly reaching up to rescue him. He worked out how the eagle could grasp the boy in its talons and beak without hurting him, and how to show Ganymede's anguished expression of fear. In order to simplify the drama of the kidnap, Rembrandt excluded the parents from the painting and concentrated all his attention on the eagle and the boy.

The power of the painting is enhanced by the strong light falling on the helpless, semi-naked urinating Ganymede as he is carried upwards by the eagle's huge outspread wings that are back-lit by a flash of lightning. The eagle's wings are menacing here, not supportive as in Rubens' eagle, and the eye of this eagle is not benign. The struggling, crying boy is a heavy burden and Zeus' eagle has to use all its strength to hold on and take him up to the god. According to one version of the story, Ganymede was made immortal by Zeus who placed him in the firmament as the constellation Aquarius. Until one learns of this, the scene evokes concern for the safety of the child and is emotive in arousing sympathy for his distress. There could hardly be a greater contrast in the psychological and emotional approach to the painting of the same subject, than these two interpretations of *The Rape of Ganymede*. This is enhanced by our looking up at Rembrandt's scene, which is out of reach of anyone, whereas Rubens' beautiful and much tamer eagle is nearer to the viewer.

Roelandt Savery

born Courtrai 1576, died Utrecht 1639

A Forest Landscape with Birds by a Lake with Ruins

oil on panel

27.3 x 38.8 cm. Rafael Valls, London

Roelandt's father, Jakob, was a distinguished landscape and animal painter, and so was his elder brother, Jakob, with whom he studied and then accompanied to Amsterdam c.1591. He was trained in the tradition of Pieter Brueghel the elder, in whose style his early works were painted.

His first commissions were painted in France for Henry IV. After his return to the Low Countries he was invited to Prague by Rudolph II, in whose service he passed the greater part of his life, travelling much in the Tyrol at the command of the Emperor to make drawings of the scenery. His drawings were engraved. The mountain views provided inspiration for Savery's naturalistic landscapes which he used as backgrounds to paint animals in natural settings. For this purpose, he was also given the opportunity to draw the animals in the Emperor's zoological gardens.

Following the death of Rudolph in 1612, he spent several years in Vienna, Munich and Salzburg before returning to Amsterdam, then spending a time in Haarlem and finally settling in Utrecht where he died, a madman, in 1639.

Savery was one of the first painters in Holland to paint pictures whose main, or only, theme was animals. He had Gillis de Hondecoeter as a pupil, and after them came two or three generations of superb Dutch and Flemish animal painters. They worked during the golden age of painting in the Low Countries, the seventeenth

1. Bustard 2. Pigeon 3. Crane 4. Bittern 5. Salmon-crested cockatoo 6. Blue and gold macaw
7. Scarlet macaw 8. Heron 9. Ostrich 10. Cassowary 11. Turkey 12. Crowned crane 13. Swan
14. Ducks 15. Swan 16. Egret 17. Heron 18. Geese 19. Domestic cock 20. Mute swan
21. Ostrich

century, which produced the geniuses, Rembrandt, Vermeer, Rubens and a host of masters, such as Melchior de Hondecoeter, Fabritius, van Dyck, Cuyp and at least another eight hundred minor masters.

Savery's canvases were usually medium sized, like the painting shown here. Most of his pictures are both signed and dated. Though his canvases were not large, the landscapes on them appear vast and are thickly populated with mammals and birds, or just birds. These were both domestic and wild birds, combined in a most unusual mixture, and yet he managed to make the scene harmonious. It is always worth scrutinizing a Savery picture for the unusual species that he drew in the menagerie, for there is frequently a bird not previously represented on panel or canvas. He was also a very good flower painter and particularly enjoyed introducing irises among other well-painted flowers in his work.

The subjects that he chose for his paintings were deliberately selected to permit him to include a large number of mammals and birds, *Orpheus Charming the Animals, Paradise, The Creation of the Birds, The Garden of Eden*, being among his mythological and religious titles, but he also abandoned any pretence at painting these subjects and many of his canvases are described merely as *Landscape with Birds* or just *Birds*.

This *Forest Landscape* is a typical Savery painting with a considerable number of bird species busily going about their normal business of feeding, displaying, grooming, flying, climbing, or running. He skilfully places birds with bright red in their plumage in different parts of the picture, as highlights in the overall composition. All bird artists were now including the red macaw for this reason, but the red facial wattles of turkeys, cockerels and crowned cranes, and the neck wattles of cassowaries also provide spots of bright colour. The orange beaks of mute swans and crests of cockatoos, are also utilised.

Savery would have painted the cassowary in Emperor Rudolph's menagerie. The first living specimen had been brought to Europe in 1597 from the Moluccas by Dutch spice traders. They are hardy birds, native to northern Australia, Papua New Guinea and adjacent islands.

Cockatoos were not new, for Mantegna had depicted a white cockatoo in his *Madonna della Vittoria*, painted about 1496. The birds of paradise, among the most ornate and colourful birds in the world, were now becoming so familiar in Europe as to feature in many bird artists' canvases. They too had originally been secured in the Moluccas, by Spanish traders in 1522. The skins had reached there by natives trading rarities from New Guinea. Savery usually placed birds of paradise at the top of his pictures, flying close to heaven.

The crowned crane is one of the most spectacular birds of Africa, with a bristling straw-coloured crest, bare pink and white cheeks, and black crown. Its nuptial dance is a wonderful exhibition of athletic leaps and dancing movements. Its presence graces any bird collection, whether in a zoo or in a picture.

Roelandt Savery

Landscape with Birds
oil on copper, 42 x 57 cm, signed and dated 1628
Kunsthistorisches Museum, Vienna

Savery's *Landscape with Birds*, 1628, was painted when he was in Utrecht, sixteen years after Emperor Rudolph II had died and Savery had left Prague, so that he no longer had access to the menagerie there. He must have relied on his sketches of the different birds in order to compose this picture.

Once more, he used a Swiss-type landscape, with a church and castle high above a valley that had a stream in the bottom. Landscapes with weirdly shaped rocks and some ruins had featured in the work of the Flemish artist Brueghel the Elder and Gillis van Coninxloo, but Savery adopts them as wild backgrounds in which to place birds at different strategic levels.

The (griffon?) vulture is a surprising addition in this painting. Savery might well have seen a vulture soaring while on his travels, but sketching in the field was not then practiced. In consequence, he appears to have made a careful sketch of the bird when perched in an aviary. He then painted this up in the sky — having first removed the perch. Without the aid of a camera, it was almost impossible to paint birds flying with any semblance of reality. The eye is not quick enough to note the posture, position of the legs, line of the body, angle of wings and action of the tail in relation to speed and whether the bird is turning, or alighting. For centuries, birds that were depicted flying may have been acceptable at the time they were painted, but they look wrong to our eyes. This is because we are accustomed now both to seeing photographs of birds frozen in flight and the results of modern

1. Goose 2. Heron 3. Blue and gold macaw 4. Scarlet macaw 5. Bustard 6. Turkey
7. Peacock 8. Crowned crane 9. Egret 10. Pelican 11. Mallard 12. Mute swan 13. Dodo
14. Heron 15. Cassowary 16. Blue and gold macaw 17. Scarlet macaw 18. Domestic cock
19. Ostriches 20. Spoonbill 21. Vulture 22. Birds of paradise

Tenniel's drawing of the dodo from Alice's Adventures in Wonderland.

artists' work when they have used photography to paint flying birds correctly.

Savery has placed a pair of pelicans on the stream at the foot of the mountain. Pelicans had been known for a very long time and revered for the ancient belief that they fed their young on their own blood, obtained by puncturing their breasts with their beaks. This led to their becoming symbols of Christ's suffering, also of charity and piety in medieval heraldry. For Savery's contemporaries to see two live birds on water in a natural setting, without any overtones of symbolism, must have been refreshing, though perhaps a little startling.

The most interesting species in this picture is, without doubt, the dodo. It was drawn from live specimens in Prince Maurice of Nassau's celebrated menagerie. Savery made at least eight studies of dodos, so fascinated was he by these incredible birds. In 1627 an Englishman, Sir Thomas Herbert, visited Mauritius, the island five hundred miles (800km) west of Madagascar, where the dodo lived. He described the bird, 'her body is round and fat, few weigh less than fifty pound, are reputed of more for wonder then (or, than) for food; greasie stomackes may seeke after them, but to the delicate, they are offensive and of no nourishment'. Sir Thomas's verbal description was accompanied by a small pen drawing, and both suggest Savery's pictures of the dodo were true to life. Recently, scientists have implied that the fatness was a seasonal condition, the birds being much slimmer at different times of the year.

The Portuguese were the first to visit Mauritius and report a bird called a Do Do. When the Dutch colonised Mauritius in 1644, the dodo's total lack of fear of man and flightless condition were its downfall. Hundreds were clubbed to death to provide fresh meat (even though repeatedly stated to be unpalatable) for sailors calling there during the long voyage to the East Indies. With the deliberate introduction of dogs and cats, and the unwitting admittance of rats, when the island was colonised, the flightless dodos had no way of escaping their pursuers, man or beast. By 1680, just fifty years after Savery took such delight in painting them, they were extinct. Nearly every picture of a dodo that was painted subsequently was derived from Savery's studies. This includes the delightful Tenniel drawing for Lewis Carroll's *Alice's Adventures in Wonderland*.

Gillis Claeszoon de Hondecoeter
born Antwerp c.1580, died Amsterdam 1638

An Assembly of Birds
oil on panel, 29.2 x 42.5 cm. Courtesy of Richard Green

Gillis de Hondecoeter was a painter of domestic fowl and other birds with landscape backgrounds, pleasantly coloured, and carefully finished. His father, the Marquis of Westerloo, in Belgium, was expatriated on account of his Protestant religion. He took refuge in Amsterdam, where he was supported by the talent of Gillis, who had painted in his leisure for his own amusement when they lived in Belgium. Gillis was the father of Gysbert and the father-in-law of J B Weenix, two artists of great ability who instructed Melchior de Hondecoeter, the greatest of all the de Hondecoeter family of painters.

Gillis de Hondecoeter painted a large number of compositions with animals, and may be compared with Roelandt Savery in this, and also in his choice of subjects. Both men repeatedly painted *Noah's Ark* and *Orpheus Charming the Animals*. In addition, these artists favoured rocky landscapes with old, gnarled trees with twisted roots which they painted with yellowish green tones. Gillis also painted a famous picture of the dodo that is now owned by the Duke of Northumberland.

Gillis de Hondecoeter's *An Assembly of Birds* is very reminiscent of similar collections of birds from South America, Africa and the Moluccas, combined with native Netherlandish species, by Roelandt Savery. The spacing and the arrangement of the birds are like Savery's but de Hondecoeter is less careful of the relative size of different elements in his picture, for example, the oak tree is young, but still too small in comparison with the birds in its branches.

1. Geese 2. Heron 3. Spoonbill 4. Crowned crane 5. Domestic cock hen 6. Turkey 7. Ostrich
8. Cassowary 9. Crowned crane 10. Kite 11. Blue and gold macaw 12. Scarlet macaw
13. Birds of paradise 14. Golden eagle 15. Egret 16. Ostrich 17. Great bustard 18. Swans
19. Pelicans 20. Cormorant 21. White peacock 22. Mallard 23. Gannet

He has tried very hard to put life into all his birds, from the birds of paradise high in the sky down through the picture to the central pool in the foreground. Each bird swimming on the pool has its shadow reflected in the water from strong backlighting. This is an imaginative and rare feature not only in paintings of this period, but much later.

All the birds in the air are ascending or descending, and this seems a common factor in paintings of this period where there are few birds in level flight. The artists appear not to have known how to position birds in flight and are especially at a loss as to what to do with their feet and legs. There is, however, one remarkable example of careful observation in the way de Hondecoeter has painted the gannet plunging into the sea just behind the white peacocks. The gannet makes a spectacular dive, only folding its wings at the last moment, so that it enters the water shaped like a torpedo and moving with similar velocity.

There is so much activity in the air that it takes a little while to see what is occurring in the foreground. De Hondecoeter has placed nearly all his white birds where the plumage will glisten as it catches the light. His white birds include cranes, a white stork, pair of pelicans, and many swans. The exception is the spoonbill, which is in the company of a heron, crowned crane and some geese on the left. Above them are more domestic fowl and a turkey. The cassowary on top of the hill, with its helmet and colourful neck silhouetted against a pale sky, is looking out of the picture, an unusual touch. An ostrich, standing tall and flapping its wings, makes a pair of bustards behind it to appear quite small birds in comparison. Nearby there is a curassow with a curly crest.

It is very rare for seabirds to be included in these early paintings of birds, but both the cormorant and gannets are featured here. Perhaps the oddest bird in this painting is the ostrich on the left. Is it sitting or falling down? Finally, there is an eagle which is so unlikely to gain enough height or speed in this crouched or perched position that it poses no threat to the two macaws, a scarlet and a blue and gold, engrossed in their own quarrel.

This is a most intriguing picture with a charm of its own derived from a certain naïvety, a delicacy of touch, delightful play of light, and the number of unusual species of birds.

Frans Snyders
born Antwerp 1579, died Antwerp 1657

The Hawk and the Hen
oil on canvas
Museum of Fine Arts, Budapest

Snyders has painted an action picture, *The Hawk and the Hen*, that shows his powers of observation and keen awareness of the behaviour of birds. This is not just a picture for art lovers, it is a carefully constructed study of bird psychology. Setting the scene on the brow of a hill, with a sweeping view of distant fields, brings the action close to the viewer while giving a feeling of this being but a small event in the wide scheme of nature. It is intense for the moment, but not over-important. Life will continue whatever the outcome of this encounter.

The brown female sparrowhawk is painted against a sky when soft sunlight is gradually spreading over the hills just after dawn. The light falls on the underwing and body of the bird which Snyders has painted in superb detail, even to the thigh of the leg that is hidden under the tail feathers. We can believe that this bird is genuinely flying, a remarkable feat of painting at this date. The hawk has alarmed the hen who must protect seven chickens that are not yet fully feathered and are unable to fly. Five chicks are aware of the danger and trying to get to mother to shelter under her wings, while two others are so intent on some other business they are conducting that they are as yet unconcerned.

Every bird can alter its shape to some degree. When it reaches out for food, it becomes slim and elongated. Should it be feeling the cold, it becomes dumpy as it squats down over its feet to prevent heat loss through the skin, and with feathers fluffed out to trap more warm air round its body for insulation. When angry, it will puff out its feathers in order to make itself look as large and intimidating as possible. The mother hen has adopted this last, threatening posture, and is as large as physically possible, even to the gaping beak.

The chickens are instinctively trying to fly, that being the quickest way to reach shelter. The one nearest the hawk seems in two minds, to run or fly, others are running and using their small wings to add some speed. What is remarkable about the way Snyders has painted these chickens, is his knowledge of how the feathers grow on a young bird that is losing its down and where the skin would show through the still very thin covering of short feathers. We can see this best along the spine of the chick in the foreground with its back to us where the wide spread of wings opens this area to view. It is less obvious, nevertheless present, where the pink skin shows through the fine covering of white feathers on the breasts.

There is a nice twist to this story of an early morning raid. Behind the hen there is another small bird which has just taken off and is flying. This is a sparrow and could well be the object of the sparrowhawk's stoop, but the hen is unaware of this. The sparrowhawk would snatch one of her chickens, given half a chance, so her alarm is justified whichever of the small birds proves to be the target. However, the hen's aggressive posture and determination to resist the attack combined with the confusing number of small birds from which to choose a meal, will probably result in the hawk swooping over the head of the hen and shooting up into the trees behind her.

Frans Snyders

Parrots

oil on wood, 122 x 98 cm. Musée des Beaux-Arts, Grenoble
(see also *Frontispiece*)

As a painter of animals, Frans Snyders was of the highest rank, a close friend of van Dyck, and he worked with other famous artists, Rubens in particular. He started life in the company of artists because his father was the keeper of a tavern in Antwerp frequented by members of the Guild of St Luke. He was a pupil of Van Balen and Pieter Brueghel and had many successful pupils himself, Paul de Vos (whose sister he married) and Jan Fyt among them. In Antwerp, he was at the centre of Flemish artistic activity at the turn of the century and was a leading figure for the first half of the seventeenth century.

Snyders was master of several genres. He is best known for his hunting canvases where ferocious beasts of prey face courageous dogs, but he could equally well paint magnificent flowers and garlands and other still life subjects, including the trophies of the chase and market stalls. His output was immense, but what is most interesting is his ability to paint live birds, which was well demonstrated when he gathered many species together for a *Concert of Birds*, a favourite title, or fruit with live parrots, or pictures with more detailed painting of a few birds like this *Parrots*.

Snyders' parrots are two red macaws with two blue and gold macaws, and two African grey parrots and a blue-fronted amazon. Besides these members of the parrot family, there are two red-billed toucans. When Christopher Columbus discovered the West Indies, and visited Guadaloupe and Trinidad, his sailors were the first Europeans to see macaws flying — a truly magnificent sight, for they are like brilliantly coloured arrows winging straight and smoothly through the air. They

accomplish this with a dignity, grandeur even, that is quite unlike their ungainly side-stepping along a perch.

The first macaws to be taken to Spain c.1500 were the scarlet macaw and the blue and gold macaw. They were placed in royal menageries and when later more imports became available, they were used as royal gifts, gradually spreading through Spain and Portugal, Holland and England. Such vividly coloured birds were irresistible to artists, who incorporated them in their paintings as soon as they were brought to Europe. Macaws first appeared in the trees in the *Garden of Eden* paintings, then they were used to bring life and colour to paintings of still life, either fruit or dead birds or collections of metal vessels. Snyders was a master painter of still life, and he, with his contemporary artists, perpetuated a tradition of always painting parrots live. Scores of bird species have been represented dead, but parrots are the exception. We cannot recall an example of a dead parrot in a painting.

In his painting of parrots and toucans, with two small purple-breasted cotingas (from Central America) Snyders has demonstrated his ability to create live birds without painting in too much fussy detail. He did not often concentrate all his interest on a few birds and this shows how captivated he was by this particular group. They are all feeding on apricots. Toucans, like parrots, are fruit eaters, occasionally varying their diet with insects. There are thirty-seven species of toucan, all found in the wild only in American tropical forests. Their huge bills may look cumbersome, but are extremely light in construction. Indeed, they are wonderful pieces of structural engineering, being a honeycomb of rigid fibres that provide strength with lightness inside the horny sheath. The tongue is nearly as long as the bill. In some species, the beak is the same length as the body and may be used to pick fruit otherwise hanging out of reach on a slender branch.

When first brought to Europe, one wonders which bird caused the biggest sensation, the macaw or the toucan.

Balthasar van der Ast

born Middelburg 1593/4, died Delft 1657

Still Life with Macaws

oil on canvas, 19 x 29cm
Fitzwilliam Museum, University of Cambridge

Ast is among the first Dutch/Flemish painters of still life pictures, who painted small pieces of fruit and flowers, insects and shells, in the manner of Jan Brueghel (1568-1625). He was a pupil of his brother-in-law Ambrosius Bosschaert (1573-1621) who is famous for his radially composed flower still life paintings. Ast went to work in Utrecht, where he became a member of the Guild of St Luke in 1619, and in Delft from 1632.

Ast painted a number of still lifes with a basket or bowl of fruits, sometimes adding exotic shells, vases of flowers, insects and lizards, and when he decided to include a bird, it was nearly always a member of the parrot family. He painted with a miniaturist's eye for detail, assembling his material on a table or ledge. His pictures are not immaculately arranged, like Caravaggio's *Fruit Basket*, to show the fruits to their best effect, nor is the fruit spaced out as in contemporary Spanish *bodegons* (still lifes), even more importantly, neither is Ast's fruit perfect, like theirs. He paints in the Dutch tradition, placing objects together according to their symbolic meaning, rather than artistically. This autumnal *Still Life with Macaws*, may be interpreted as ripe fruit about to perish, either by mould spots, or flies, moths and caterpillars nibbling at them. The transience of all life, including human life, is represented here.

Besides the symbolism, there is much to enjoy in this colourful, small painting, neatly signed and dated on the top step. Apart from the beautifully painted insects, the two bright red crustaceans provide a complementary touch of colour to the cherries, seeds of the opened pomegranate, red currants and the feathers of the scarlet macaw. The exquisite china bowl and plate are obviously valued possessions, perhaps once blue and white but now the blue paint has faded. The blue on the macaw's plumage has certainly dulled. Ast painted a very similar fruit still life, with these two macaws in the foreground, tails crossed, that is now in Copenhagen. The extraordinarily painstaking observation and accuracy which he applied to the fruit has not been extended to the birds. Throughout the history of bird painting, we frequently find artists who successfully paint plants, insects, fishes and shells, but are not so good at painting birds. The blue and yellow macaw with the scarlet macaw are here for their colour, and to give the painting a feeling of life (however transitory). They serve that purpose well, but neither of the greatest masters, Dürer and Caravaggio, would have misplaced the eye of the blue and yellow macaw, nor painted a black top mandible instead of the correct white upper mandible of the scarlet macaw. They would have observed the lie of the feathers, and painted the correct number of primaries and secondaries. Ast's sweeping brush strokes used to paint the tails make them more impressionistic than realistic, which is curious, coming from the hand of such a good miniaturist. Birds are infinitely more difficult to paint, combining accuracy of form with a spirit of life, than Ast, or many other artists, realised.

Ever since macaws were first brought to Europe from South America soon after Columbus discovered the New World in 1493, they have been greatly favoured by artists for their wonderful decorative qualities. They were included in the religious

paintings of Cranach and Burgkmair in the early years of the sixteenth century. Most of these first appearances of macaws in paintings are birds sitting high up in trees. Jan Brueghel the Elder painted them on several occasions, being one of the first to bring them indoors and place them on a parrot stand in a picture of the *Five Senses* when they might well have represented sound, albeit a not very pleasant one, as well as sight. Snyders found them so appealing that he made them the main motif of his picture *Parrots* (see Frontispiece). Ast is among the earliest artists to give them such prominence in a still life painting. His *Still Life with Macaws* may not be one of the greatest attempts to paint these wonderful birds, but the whole picture is very decorative, glowing with colour from the reds and yellows, and interesting from an historical point of view.

Water rail

Bitterns

Paul de Vos
born Hulst 1596 died Antwerp 1678

Bitterns, Herons and Water Rails in a Landscape
oil on canvas, 103 x 260 cm
Rafael Valls, London

Paul, and his more famous brother Cornelis, de Vos were born in the small town of Hulst in Zeeland Flanders. Hulst is notable today for its almost intact ramparts, complete with moats, bulwarks and three gates, which were built when the de Vos brothers were youths, between 1618 to 1621. The town hall has a painting, *View of Hulst*, by Cornelis de Vos, dated 1628.

Paul de Vos was a pupil of three artists, the last one being his brother-in-law, Frans Snyders, whose work greatly influenced him. He painted lively scenes of animals fighting, dogs chasing game, and trophies of the hunt. These were favourite topics for the nobility, whose fondness for falconry and hunting extended to buying pictures of game and scenes of the chase.

When he painted these subjects, his work is hard to distinguish from that of Snyders. The confusion is compounded by their practice of working together on some pictures. A slight difference lies in de Vos' preference for warmer colours, especially his light browns. He also favoured flowing, curving lines that give movement to his animal figures. Another feature of his work is the slimness of his mammals and birds. His painting varies in quality, but Rubens, a neighbouring Antwerp citizen, thought sufficiently highly of four of his pictures to own them. These were examples of de Vos' range of subjects: *Kitchen Piece with Cats Fighting, Peasants with Venison and Fruit, A Concert of Birds*, and *Fruit and Birds*.

Herons

De Vos lived in Antwerp for most of his life and became a member of the painters' guild there in 1620.

The unusually shaped canvas *Bitterns, Herons and Water Rails in a Landscape* shows many of de Vos' artistic characteristics. The landscape is flat and wet, typical Low Countries scenery, with a cloudy sky. All the birds are caught in some movement, pecking or protesting, beaks open, wings extended in alarm, or flying in to land. Because there are two birds of each species, de Vos has been able to show different views and paint the plumage from different angles. He is not a master in the use of light and shade, and has made no attempt to give us shadows that the birds' bodies ought to be casting on the ground. Nor does he show us darkened plumage where the wings should cast shadows on the body beneath their outline.

He does manage to convey the extraordinary contortions that bitterns can contrive with their long necks, and the scrawniness of herons' necks. Bitterns are birds of the reed beds, difficult to see at any time, and more often heard than seen. When hiding, the bill is pointed vertically in an elongated pose, but they walk with shoulders hunched and head lowered. In spring, their booming call may be audible up to a mile away.

Artists very rarely paint shy water rails. They skulk in reeds, feeding in the margins of pools and dislike showing themselves. To be caught out in the open like this is sufficient to unnerve any water rail, and to find a heron landing nearby would be very frightening. Their alarm is well conveyed. The slate-blue under plumage is very fine and compact, giving them a velvety look. When scuttling back into cover, they flick their tails, revealing white undertail coverts, which are clearly visible on the bird on the right. The long red bill is unusual in marsh birds and de Vos has shown that the bird has a correspondingly long tongue, which is a small detail indicative of just how observant he has been.

Water rail

69

Paul de Vos

Variety of Birds
oil on canvas
Museo Real Academia de Bellas Artes, San Fernando

Paul de Vos has painted a *Variety of Birds* from South America, Europe and New Guinea, in an extensive Flemish river landscape. The towering sky is evocative of Zeeland Flanders where large areas of the flat landscape recede into a huge sky. Against this familiar background, de Vos has placed some dead tree trunks and branches on which to perch groups of birds. Elements in the foreground are not in scale, which is a little disconcerting, but the variety of birds is so intriguing that our attention quickly becomes focused on them.

The first, most colourful group of birds is on the left. For anyone familiar with Snyders' *Parrots* at Grenoble (see Frontispiece) this part of the picture is a reminder that de Vos and Snyders were brothers-in-law who sometimes worked on the same picture. Did Snyders paint the two red macaws, two blue and gold macaws, red-billed toucan and blue-fronted amazon, all from South America, with the African grey parrot? Or did de Vos copy Snyders' *Parrots*, or were the birds all set up in a group in the studio and both men worked from the models? The macaws are very still, while nearly all the other birds in the picture are active. The right hand group all look as though they would be candidates for a picture entitled *A Concert of Birds*. The 'singing' species are (from the right) a beak of a muscovy and a whole muscovy duck, two grebes, a black male scoter (his brown female is more interested in the up-ending duck) and a dark barnacle goose with a domestic

goose. Overhead, a male red-plumed bird of paradise sails through the air toward a flying swallow and kingfisher.

The waders on the grass and mud area by the water are two lapwings, two snipes and a woodcock. The thin tree branch which is growing from the stump on which the eagle stands is far too distant in the landscape, but useful to support a fourth group of birds. De Vos has included a pair of nightingales which are very rarely included in bird pictures, with a pair of tree sparrows and chaffinches, one bullfinch and one greenfinch and an acrobatic blue titmouse. Artists frequently show the great and blue titmice in what appear to be incredible positions, hanging upside-down from small twigs, yet they have been correctly observed and painted, as anyone fortunate enough to have these enchanting little birds in their garden will know.

Without the exotics at the left, and the flying bird of paradise, this would have been an authentic Low Countries *Variety of Birds*. How much duller, though, without de Vos' (and Snyders'?) avian and artistic licence.

Gysbert Gilliszoon de Hondecoeter
born Amsterdam 1604, died Utrecht 1653

Speckled Drake
oil on wood, 33.6 x 48.7cm, Staatliche Kunsthalle, Karlsruhe

Three generations of the Dutch de Hondecoeter family painted birds, Gysbert being in the middle. His father, Gillis (died Amsterdam 1638) painted woodland scenes of a yellowish-green hue with misshapen tree-trunks and tangled roots which formed the backgrounds for animals of all kinds.

Gillis taught his own son Gysbert, who painted landscape like his father, and waterfowl and nesting hens reminiscent of some of Savery's work. Gysbert became a member of the Utrecht Guild in 1630 and went on to develop a much more realistic style, concentrating on domestic fowl. The quality of his work varied, some of the best being attributed to his famous son Melchior. Gysbert and Melchior rarely painted dead birds, but their still life pictures were works of some quality. Gysbert taught Melchior until his early death in 1653, when the youngest member of this talented family went to finish his art education with his uncle Jan Weenix. It is sad that Gysbert never saw evidence of the mature genius of Melchior, for his son became one of the best painters of decorative, lively bird pictures of all time.

There are almost certainly as many pictures of domestic fowl in existence as there are of all other bird species put together. Painting domestic birds has several advantages over trying to find and sketch wild birds. They are near at hand, either in the artist's own backyard, or a neighbour's. They do not fly away the moment that an artist wishes to paint them, in fact they are slower in their movements, often being heavier than their counterparts in the wild, apart from being pinioned. Farmyard cocks are often great characters, as well as being splendidly feathered. They rule their roost and are a delight to paint in all their arrogance and assertiveness. Domestic ducks interbreed with the mallard and produce a never-ending variety of plumage. Pictures of such familiar scenes as the barnyard with poultry

and village pond with tame geese and ducks, have always been popular and still find a ready market. In the nineteenth century, the idea was developed to include a charming female figure who was feeding the birds, and numerous goose-girls and pictures with titles such as *Feeding the Ducks* also became popular.

There is nothing pretentious about domestic ducks, but they have a certain dignity that even their waddling gait cannot destroy. Gysbert de Hondecoeter has painted an admirably simple and natural-looking *Speckled Drake*. The bird has such self-possession in its pose, and its calm dignity is conveyed by the expression of the eye. By painting a single bird with little or no background, Gysbert could so easily have made *Speckled Drake* a mere study of shape, texture and colour. It is much more than that, for it has become a picture by virtue of the sensitivity with which it was painted, so that we see it as a beautiful, living creature, which is how Gysbert saw it.

For many years, it was thought to have been the work of the master Frans Snyders. Only in the late nineteenth century was it recognised as being by G. G. de Hondecoeter. This beautiful bird portrait has the same feeling of charm and integrity as found in the painting of *The White Drake* by Joseph Crawhall c.1895.

Jan Asselyn
born Dieppe 1610, died Amsterdam 1652

The Threatened Swan
1650, oil on canvas, 144 x 171 cm, Rijksmuseum, Amsterdam

This Flemish/Dutch painter was one of a group of artists who studied in Italy and he became an important landscapist of the Italianate school. He was a Huguenot refugee from Normandy who went to Amsterdam before he set off through France to Italy, travelling as far as Rome. In 1644 he was recorded at Lyons, where artists en route to Italy often remained for a while because the city had a number of wealthy clients for their pictures. By 1647 he had returned to Amsterdam where he painted *The Threatened Swan*.

By a curious paradox, this is his most famous picture. He was essentially a landscape painter, though he also did some winter scenes and a few pictures of feathered game in the style of his friend Jan Baptist Weenix. His work is noted for his keen observation of foliage and reflections in water. After his return from Italy, his landscapes included ruins, and he used strong light and shade effects, especially when painting landscapes under a glowing yellow evening light.

The Threatened Swan is painted against a backdrop of a lake surrounded by wooded hills, with a deep yellow light behind the bird that tinges the whiteness of its outspread wings and its breast. The bird is defending its nest and eggs against an open-mouthed dog in the water. The swan's powerful feet and wings are spread wide, with beak thrust forward hissing a warning to the dog not to come any closer. The bird is so agitated that it has been flapping its wings for some time so that loose feathers are flying all round it, and one has landed to float on the water. It is an impressive painting of great power. Any person or animal would be intimidated by such a show of strength and weighty aggression. The mute swan is painted life-size, about five feet high (they are between 146 and 160 cm in length, with a wing-span of 208-238 cm). The pose is exceptionally well managed and the painting of the feathers is very well balanced between the dense body plumage, curved right wing and spread out left wing feathers like fingers.

Asselyn died two years after painting *The Threatened Swan*. In subsequent years it acquired a number of inscriptions turning it into a political allegory. It came to represent the vigilance of the Grand Pensionary, Johan de Witt (the swan) defending Holland (the nest) against the enemies of the state (the dog). Johan de Witt was a republican who opposed the Orange party.

Whether seen simply as a beautiful painting of a swan, a scene from nature, or an allegory, it is a masterly painting.

Johannes or Jan Fyt

born Antwerp 1611, died Antwerp 1661

Cocks Fighting

oil on canvas. Musée des Beaux-Arts Ancien, Brussels

With Snyders and Jan Brueghel the elder, Fyt was the leading Flemish painter of still life subjects in the seventeenth century. His work is more varied, and of smaller format than theirs. He was a master of dramatic compositions painted with a vigour and realism that create their own atmosphere. To give additional drama to his still life pictures of dead animals, he introduced a live cat or dog. He was especially fond of painting eagles and partridges, at which he excelled. His large *Eagles Feeding*, in Antwerp Museum, is considered to be one of his masterpieces. He is represented in most other major international galleries.

Fyt began his training in Antwerp about 1621-22 and then entered Snyders' studio. He learned much from Snyders and in 1629, with his help, he became a master and then travelled to Paris and Italy, where he visited Venice and Rome. He was back home in Antwerp by 1641 and married in 1654, rather late in life. The Antwerp archives record his involvement in several lawsuits. He was famous in his own lifetime and consequently was imitated and this makes attribution of some of his work uncertain. He also collaborated with other painters, e.g. with Jordaens and Bosschaert. Unlike the highly coloured work of Snyders, Fyt's palette was much more subtle, with harmonious colours skilfully blended and he added deep shadows to his subdued tones. His brushwork was freer so that live, fighting birds suited his looser style of painting better than the minuscule detail of the pure still life.

Cocks fighting have been chosen frequently by artists as subjects for a picture, but not very many can match the quality of Fyt's dramatic piece reproduced here. He has used all his skill in painting with subtle tones to create the right, closed-in atmosphere of the barnyard, where a battle for supremacy is taking place between two of nature's most belligerent birds. Supposedly tamed by man, cocks are utterly defiant of all rules when it comes to a fight. This combat is so intense that the hens, who usually keep out of the way and pretend not to notice when males start fighting, are actually joining in and making as much clamour themselves.

There is little doubt as to who is going to win this contest. The one that recognises the importance of gaining the higher ground and climbs on the back of another to achieve it, is definitely the one to get on in this world. The wonderful display of white feathers immediately takes the eye to this bird. The expression of fury in its eye is beautifully conveyed. The brown cock looks more aggrieved than angry. This bird blends in with the browns and dull reds of its surroundings, which is not suggestive of the qualities of leadership. A little touch of humour is supplied by the hen on the right. She is certainly no neutral observer.

Pictures that are not just fine paintings of birds, but also tell a story, are popular. When an artist puts his feelings into a picture and makes it clear what he is saying, the viewer can more easily respond and derive pleasure from it. This painting can be readily understood, as well as being appreciated for the skill in painting and composition. It is a masterpiece to be enjoyed on many levels.

Jan Fyt's dramatic picture of two barnyard cocks fighting for supremacy is a rare subject for him. Despite the apparently brilliant white plumage of one cock, a close examination reveals many different whites in his feathers, just as there are many subtle tones of soft browns in the feathers of his rival. Fyt was a virtuoso in the manner in which he used light brushwork to create subtle contrasts of light and shade, as well as varying depth of colours. He has also produced a work with great atmosphere.

Nicolas Robert

born Langres 1614, died Paris 1685

Blue Peacock Displaying

watercolour on vellum, 38.8 x 31.2 cm
Christie's Images, London

Robert was the greatest French natural history artist of the seventeenth century, famous for his watercolours of plants and birds painted on fine vellum. He was the son of an innkeeper, who learned to paint and to engrave. He spent two years in Italy, where he published a set of botanical engravings with the help of Giovanni Battista de Rossi. When he returned to France in 1640 his talent was quickly recognised and he was employed by Gaston, Duke of Orléans to paint the most unusual and rarest animals in the royal menagerie. He also painted plants, and when the Duke died, his collection of paintings, or *vélins*, became the property of Louis XIV. Robert produced 727 paintings on leaves of vellum of which 252 represented birds. They had little or no background details and only slight hints at the sort of habitat where the bird might be found. The collection became the basis of the *vélins* that are now in the Natural History Museum in Paris. Louis XIV commissioned Robert to continue with his work and to make engravings from his drawings. In 1666 he was appointed painter of miniatures to the king, contracted to produce a minimum of fifty-four *vélins* a year and above this quota he was paid on a pro-rata basis. Robert achieved his target, and more, by presiding over a workshop. His botanical subjects were supplied by the Jardin des Plantes in Paris, and the birds by the menagerie at Versailles. Robert worked on other series of bird drawings and paintings, with backgrounds and foregrounds of plants, including this picture of a blue peacock.

As may be expected with such a large output, the quality of the *vélins* varies. The best of Robert's show his overwhelming concern for scientific accuracy and immense powers of observation. Robert had a distinctive technique. He used short, very fine lines that can only have been applied with a brush of few hairs, and small spots of watercolour. The train of the peacock demonstrates this method of working very clearly. His watercolours look as fresh as the day he painted them. This peacock glows with colour and he captures the proud, strutting bird in full display, reminding one of the expression 'as proud as a peacock'.

The peacock is the most flamboyant member of a very glamorous family of birds, the pheasants. It has been semi-domesticated for centuries, but in the wild the birds are natives of India and Ceylon. It was known to the ancient Greeks and Romans who made it part of their mythologies as a favourite bird of Juno. Its delicately-flavoured flesh was served up at banquets, the meat being decorated with the head and some of the feathers. In an age when spices were required both to preserve meat and to disguise the taste of bad meat, the curious fact that peacock flesh remained untainted for a very long time was quickly translated into a sign. It was assumed that the peacock's flesh was incorruptible and so it became a symbol of the resurrection. Countless Italian religious paintings have a peacock prominently positioned, representing the immortality of Christ. The long ornamental feathers that make such a wonderful, almost circular display, are elongated upper tail coverts growing from the bird's back. The train of the male bird does not reach its fullest length until its sixth year. In the train there are between one hundred and 150 feathers. A mature male is 203 x 228.6 cm (80 to 92 in.) in length, including the train. He moults in July and his new train is rarely complete before winter.

Paolo Porpora

born Naples 1617, died Rome 1673

Still Life with Little Owl, Black-winged Stilt and Quails

oil on canvas, 74 x 99 cm
Musée du Louvre, Paris

Porpora was one of the few Italian painters of the seventeenth century to specialise in still life. Few of his pictures have survived and most of these are of fruits and flowers, with birds or small insects or frogs.

Porpora worked at Naples before moving to Rome in 1656. He became a member of the Academy of St Luke where he joined other artists who were followers of Caravaggio, painting in his style with extreme exactness and paying great attention to light and shade. His colours were delicate, as shown by the beautiful roses in this painting.

Apart from the roses, the main feature of Porpora's *Still Life with Little Owl, Black-winged Stilt and Quails*, is the black and white bird on the right with the improbably long legs. The Black-winged stilt is a marsh bird, probing in the mud with its long red bill as it feeds on insects, molluscs, worms, tadpoles and frogs. Porpora may not have known of this last item in the stilt's diet when he painted the small frog on the stone by the pool. The stilt is only 38.1 cm (15in.) in length and, when it flies, its red legs project between 16.5 to 17.8 cm (6½-7in.) beyond its tail. On the ground, the bird always appears to be precariously balanced on these extraordinary legs and it walks very deliberately with long graceful strides. In England it was called a long-legged plover until the bird artist Prideaux John Selby saw Thomas Bewick's description of the bird and his wood engraved tailpiece showing a man walking on stilts. Selby combined the two ideas and in 1833 renamed the bird black-winged stilt, a name that we still use. It is not often seen in Britain, but it has bred here a few times. The inclusion of a black-winged stilt, very rarely seen in pictures, makes this painting special.

The little owl peering out from the back of this picture is present in many other bird paintings. Owls were feared in the middle ages, and many people still regard them with superstitious dislike. This is because the owl's luminous eyes, its ability to remain awake all night and to see in the dark, seemed to indicate supernatural powers. However, it was revered as sacred to Athene, the Greek goddess who could see in darkness, and its image was stamped on Athenian silver coins which were called 'owls of Laurium' (because minted from the silver mines at Laurium near Athens). In still life paintings, an owl's associations with darkness and death conveyed the idea of the transience of life. The species in this picture is the little owl, which was introduced into Northamptonshire, England, from Holland in 1889 and has since spread over most of the country.

The three small dumpy birds are quails, only 17.8 cm (7in.) in length, and another rarity in Britain, though Porpora would be familiar with it as a table bird and the source of small but delicious eggs.

Porpora has chosen a modestly coloured group of still life objects to paint. He has explored the effect of water on pebbles, making them shiny and very tactile. He carefully painted the bird feathers, the knobbly skin of the frog, the delicate petals of the roses, and the chalky wings of the brimstone butterfly to show different natural textures. The quails and frog are warming themselves in the sun, while the owl has sought the shade. The whole is painted in a subtle blend of cool and warmer colours, with a touch of blue added just as you would find it when walking round a garden. This still life picture is an outdoor scene of great intimacy and charm, quite unlike either landscape pictures with birds, or the arrangements of still life objects on tables indoors. Its special qualities are probably the reason for a work by such a little known artist being hung in the Louvre.

Carel Fabritius
born Midden Beemster 1622, died Delft 1654

The Goldfinch
oil on panel, 33.5 x 22.8 cm, signed and dated 1654
Courtesy Mauritshuis, The Hague

This charming picture of *The Goldfinch, Het Putterje*, was acquired in 1896 for the Mauritshuis by its director Dr A. Bredius, and has become the hallmark of this gallery, which is noted for the fine quality of all its paintings. It is the work of Carel Fabritius whose life was cut short as a result of an explosion at an arms store in Delft. He had lived in Delft for four years, and painted *The Goldfinch* there in the year that he died. It is one of only eight paintings that can be definitely ascribed to Fabritius. He was born in a village just north of Amsterdam and, for a short time, 1641-43, was one of Rembrandt's pupils. Far from being overawed by the great master, he reversed Rembrandt's practice in that he painted dark objects against a light background. Following his period with Rembrandt, he lost his wife and two children. When he remarried he went to live in Delft.

Just why he chose to paint a goldfinch is not known and has been the subject of much conjecture. '*Het Putter*' is the Dutch name of the goldfinch and it may have been connected with the surnames Potter and de Putter, of both an acquaintance and a friend of Fabritius. Putter, literally translated, is 'drawer of water', and this name was also used in England as a vernacular term, a 'draw-water', for pet goldfinches. As a pet bird, it was ideal in that it sang pleasantly, was relatively long-lived (up to seven years), and easily fed because it eats grain. A small bucket or pot of water, if suspended on a chain, presented no problems to a goldfinch who dexterously pulled up the pot, safely stowing the loops of chain under one foot while hauling in with the other foot, hence the term 'draw-water'.

Cage-birds were, and still are, far more popular as pets in Continental European countries than in Britain. Every Dutch child hankered after a pet bird. In most of the pictures of Dutch interiors, there are cages, suspended from the ceiling, attached to a wall, or on a stand. It is not uncommon to find the occupant to be a goldfinch. Fabritius's pet bird is secured to its perch by a light chain.

None of this is in the least remarkable, but this picture is regarded as so remarkable that it has been called the finest bird painting of all time or, perhaps more truthfully, the finest bird painting until this century. In a wider context, it is seen as an oustanding example of the virtuosity and excellence of painting in the Golden Age of Dutch and Flemish painting. If we think of it in more modest terms, it is one of the most attractive of all Dutch seventeenth century paintings because of the deft execution, the simplicity, and command of perspective. It was certainly unusual to paint a single bird and to make it the sole subject of a picture.

Fabritius has created the illusion that the bird is standing there, momentarily turned our way, but about to move. The bird seems to be alive, its living presence assured by the perfect rendering of the face and eye in this half turned position. Technically, the illusion is created by the strong shadow to the right of the bird. To use so few, bold, strokes in an age of miniaturist painting of still life was most unusual. It was not until two centuries had passed that another bird painter of equal stature, Josef Wolf, could demonstrate that it is as important to know what to leave out as what to paint in. Fabritius has gauged that perfectly and we have a bird in suspended animation, exactly as we would see it in real life.

Pieter Boel

born Antwerp 1622, died Paris 1674

An Assembly of Birds and Mammals in a Landscape

oil on canvas, 172 x 292.2 cm
Courtesy Richard Green Gallery

Pieter Boel was an excellent painter of birds, mammals, flowers and fruit. He was a pupil of Frans Snyders, after learning the rudiments of painting and engraving from his father, Jan Boel. He may also have been taught by Jan Fyt whom he imitated. He visited Italy, where he went to Genoa to work with his uncle Cornelis de Wael, and was in Rome for a time. On his return to Antwerp he was admitted a master of the guild in 1650. Later in his career, he went to Paris and worked with the French artist Le Brun for the Gobelins tapestry factory, from about 1668, and as court painter to Louis XIV.

Pieter Boel's still life pictures are numerous, and include dead game pieces and kitchen scenes resembling those of Jan Fyt, who had made these very popular in the 1630s and 1640s. Although Boel's work was similar in composition, like this example of a crowded scene of animals, he used broader brush strokes and less bright colours than Fyt. When painting feathers, he laid down an area of colour, then an impression of the feathers on top so that the shape and form are present, but not much detail or close finishing. Boel also liked theatrical lighting, such as

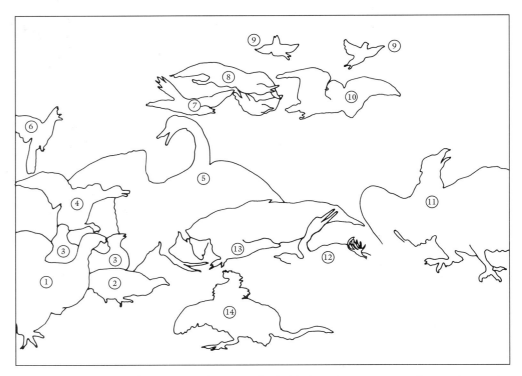

1. Turkey 2. Albino pheasant 3. Pheasant 4. Sheldrake 5. Swan, mute 6. Jay 7. Magpie
8. Red-breasted merganser 9. Kingfisher 10. Short-eared owl 11. Golden eagle 12. Heron
13. Peacock 14. Domestic cock

the bright sunny day when he gathered together this *Assembly of Birds and Mammals in a Landscape* and painted them on a very large canvas.

This lively scene is unusual in Boel's work, in that all the animals, including some ten species of birds, are alive, though there are so many quarrels taking place, that one fears that situation will not hold much longer.

Boel is a master at painting fur, hence his bringing the bear, donkey or mule, stag, boar and fox into the picture on the right, and the wild cat scrambling up a tree on the left (to the consternation of a flying jay). Another unusual feature is the golden eagle, both on the defensive as well as on the attack, for the dog is clearly uncomfortable with the eagle's talons digging into its back. Most artists just show the eagle in the ascendancy, without a foe to make them fear. Even the red squirrel is objecting to the perfectly innocuous tortoise. The swan and the sheldrake are hissing, the red-breasted merganser, magpie, jay and kingfishers are mobbing the short-eared owl, and the farmyard cockerel is pinioned by the fox. The turkey and two pheasants may be mere onlookers, but the albino pheasant has a wary eye on the fox. What a mêlée, and how far removed is the mood of this painting from the earlier Flemish artists' peaceful Garden of Eden pictures. It is a great piece of painting, but not a very pleasant scene.

Boel has created a compositional problem by including species of such disparate size, even though he is working on a large scale. Nevertheless, from the huge bear to the small tortoise, he maintains the correct size relationship.

Like other recorders of natural history subjects, Boel found albino birds fascinating. The unusual and bizarre animal forms, whether albinos lacking in any colour, or very dark, almost black melanistic forms, were prized among collectors and given a prominent place in pictures. The albino pheasant is not uncommon, nor is partial albinism where only some of the feathers are lacking in their true colour pigments.

Jan Steen

born Leiden 1626, died Leiden 1679

The Poultry Yard

oil on canvas, 108 x 82.5 cm, signed and dated 1660
Courtesy Mauritshuis, The Hague

Jan Steen was the son of a wealthy brewer and was fortunate in being encouraged by his father, who recognised his early talent as an artist. He became the pupil of Adriaen van Ostade at Haarlem and then Jan van Goyen at The Hague, as well as studying at the academy at Leiden. He had great natural technical facility which allowed him to turn to any subject. While practising as an artist, he was also director of a brewery at Delft for a while, and several other businesses, but he found the combination of running a business and painting too difficult. He preferred to paint. Perhaps the best outcome of his business experience was his participation in the founding of the painters' Guild of St Luke (the patron saint of artists) at Leiden in 1648. The Painters' Guilds set standards of training in technical accomplishment and taught the young artist the necessary disciplines to enable him to paint realistically on panel or canvas. Being admitted as a member of the guild, following an apprenticeship and submission of a masterpiece, was the mark of acceptance into the circle of master painters. The Golden Age of Dutch and Flemish painting in the seventeenth century coincided with the period when the guild system flourished in Holland and Antwerp.

Sometimes Steen was successful in business, on other occasions he was in debt. Despite all the vicissitudes, he painted over seven hundred pictures, many of them masterpieces. His subjects were taken from the everyday life of the peasantry and merchants in a variety of styles to suit his tavern scenes or interiors of respectable households. Steen's bird paintings reflect his versatility. In the Rijksmuseum, Amsterdam there is a very good interior with a woman feeding a parrot. He did several outdoor scenes such as poultry yards, and a dovecot (Paris, Institut Néerlandais). Besides these pastorals, he painted the less pleasant aspects of life with a cock fight at an inn (in the museum Bergen op Zoom).

In 1660, Steen painted *The Poultry Yard*, a subject that has been very popular throughout the history of painting. This particular yard, however, is far removed from the usual cottage poultry yard with a few hens and ducks. This yard is a courtyard belonging to the stately mansion we can see through the arch. It is crowded with many different kinds of fowl which have servants especially assigned to look after them. The pigeon loft has space for many domestic birds, and there are several breeds of turkeys, geese and ducks. The stream has a plank across and a shallow side for ease of access to the ducks and geese. The peacock has come in from the garden, adding a touch of opulence to the scene.

The Poultry Yard is a masterpiece of composition, a delight in the use of paint and colour to show form and texture, but, perhaps it is more than that. It may be a social comment or, quite simply, a record of a scene chanced on by Steen. The servant with torn coat cradles a hen in his arm and carries a basketful of small chickens. He, and the other servant are watching the girl with expressions of indulgent tenderness. The girl has cast her hat on one side to get down to the serious business of feeding the lamb, perfectly assured of her welcome in the yard. This is a scene where all the people in it are showing their care and concern for the birds, the lamb, and for one another. Kindliness pervades this picture.

Govert Dirkszoon Camphuysen

born Gorkum 1623, died Amsterdam 1672

Poultry

oil on canvas
City of York Art Gallery

Camphuysen was a Dutch painter of landscapes with flocks and herds, portraits and a few pictures of brooding hens. His painting style was realistic, the result of acute powers of observation and a very particular technique. His animal paintings were so close in style and composition to Paulus Potter that their work has been confused. His extensive landscapes, with carefully spaced isolated trees and some cattle and herdsmen, have been passed off as the work of Aelbert Cuyp. Only his portraits, done in Stockholm for the Swedish court between 1652 and 1663, have been unequivocally labelled as his work.

When in Holland, he worked in Amsterdam where he married on 9 February 1647 and acquired citizenship on 16 March 1650. He returned to Amsterdam, from Sweden, a little after November 1663. His pictures of hens are very rare, and usually depict brooding hens. This picture of *Poultry* includes a hen house, but the poultry are outside, painted in close proximity to the artist and thus the viewer of the picture, and rather too large for their setting.

This picture is thoroughly Dutch, with no hint of Italianate influences. The solid wooden planks of the building, flat countryside and dull grey wintry sky are painted with a palette of greys, browns and ochres. These are subtly blended and balanced, with the lichen-covered tree on one side and the sky on the other. The birds have sought out the shafts of sunlight for warmth, and the sun reflects the ochre tints in their white plumage. It is a remarkably simple composition, and the birds are completely natural. There is no drama here, no story even. The effect is to make the viewer take an interest in the textures, which are very beautifully painted. The roughness of the wood, delicacy of the lichen on the bark of the tree, and very distinctive plumage with the irregularly placed black feathers among the white of the main cockerel attract attention. Of secondary interest, the bird pecking the ground, is not only in the shade but also plumaged in all the deeper shades of the artist's chosen palette. The eyes of this bird have very small highlights, in contrast with the bright glint in the eye of the prominent bird who is seen in the sunshine. Camphuyzen has not been tempted to over-emphasize the red wattles for any striking effect. He has kept these completely in proportion in strength of tone.

Camphuyzen's *Poultry* is a uniquely Dutch painting, whose subtleties of tone and texture give it its great character and integrity in observation and execution.

Francis Barlow
born 1626, died London 1704

Landscape With a Green Woodpecker, a Jay, Two Pigeons, a Redstart, a Lizard and Two Frogs
oil on canvas, 76.2 x 63.6 cm, c.1650
Yale Center for British Art, Paul Mellon Collection

Barlow was one of a circle of artists whose love of animals prompted them to specialise in painting scenes where they formed the main motif. There were Dutch artists working in England whom he must have known, like Abraham Hondius (in London by 1674) and Jan Griffier (in London soon after 1666), and the fact that there were so many etchers, including Wenceslaus Hollar, who could interpret his designs of fables, or small scenes for sets of prints, must have influenced him.

Barlow painted many pictures, some simple, like the close view of the jay and other birds, others with large landscapes that gave an impression of England before industry spoilt so much of the countryside. Under these circumstances, his species were native birds, waterfowl, kingfishers, herons, birds of prey and game birds, including bustards that then inhabited East Anglia. When he wished to paint foreign species he went to Ham House where the Earl of Lauderdale had a magnificent aviary, c.1678. Alternatively, he could take a stroll in St James's Park in central London where Charles II had a large collection of birds. Barlow sketched ostriches there, that had been presented by the Moroccan Ambassador in 1681, also cassowaries. Charles' mews held many birds of prey and Barlow's pictures included some fine peregrines and eagles. He used these for action pictures, and dogs barking at waterfowl also were used to provoke movement. When required to provide sporting pictures, he was master of the situation and his excellence in this genre encouraged the English taste for paintings and prints of sporting scenes that was to dominate British bird painting in the next two centuries.

Barlow could capture, most convincingly, the form and delicate colouring of wood pigeons, as seen in this picture. Painting a bird head-on to the viewer demands a keen appreciation of foreshortening and Barlow has got the woodpigeon in just the position, head correctly held, prior to pecking at some speck of food on the ground. He is equally observant of the green woodpecker, two claws forward, two pointing backwards and using the special stiff shafts of the tail to brace itself in an upright position against the trunk of the tree. The bright-eyed redstart, although in the shade, is beautifully painted to show the rusty red of its tail that gives it its name. However, the most spectacular bird here is the flying jay, with its soft pink plumage, and blue in the wing patches. He almost certainly had seen this in the wild, even though he painted it from a specimen. It is a very believable picture of a jay taking off in flight.

One of the hallmarks of a good bird painter is his ability to paint the eyes correctly, to give life to the picture. The small highlight is the vital spark that brings the bird alive. Barlow is particularly good at painting the eyes of all these birds.

Francis Barlow

An Ostrich and a Cassowary

oil on canvas, 194.5 x 133.4cm
Courtesy Christopher Gibbs, London

Francis Barlow is Britain's first bird artist whose work could compare with continental artists and he remained the best British animal artist for many years afterwards. He was the first native English bird book illustrator and professional etcher, also landscape painter, of any note. His drawing and composition were very good, and he managed to capture the spirit and character of his birds. He painted in oil on canvas, and did many line drawings, some of which he afterwards tinted.

It is not certain where Barlow was born. From the manner in which he paints broad flat landscapes, it has long been thought he came from Lincolnshire, but one of his sets of published prints includes the information 'Indigenam Londinensem'. In 1650 he had completed his apprenticeship and was elected a member of the Painter-Stainers' Company. Two years later, he was in a studio in Drury Lane, painting animals that he obviously had observed very carefully, and knew intimately. He became famous for his pictures of 'fowl and birds and colours them from the life'. He was said to paint the eye first, and then work outwards from that point of reference.

When Barlow painted two very large exotic birds, the cassowary and ostrich, he took as his models some live birds in St James's Park, London, where Charles II had a collection of birds. Charles frequently strolled in the park, fed the deer and visited his bird menagerie. He insisted that his subjects also be allowed to wander freely in the park and this made his courtiers very fearful for his safety. However, Charles' generosity in sharing the park made him very popular and Barlow was only one of many Londoners and foreign visitors who took advantage of the opportunity to see rare birds in cages and around the lake.

That an ostrich was a bird with strange nesting habits and could run very fast, had been known in England for centuries before it was seen in the flesh. The Old English name, *steorc* and its variant *ostrice* had entered the language c.1225 by way of the Bible, where it is mentioned ten times in the Old Testament as a bird with which the Jews were familiar. Another four centuries passed before live specimens were seen in England.

In November 1681, the Moroccan ambassador set out on a peace mission at the head of a caravan of two hundred horsemen taking presents for the King of England, including two lions and twenty ostriches. When the ambassador was received by the King and Queen in the Whitehall banqueting house, he and his retinue caused much astonishment by their strange costume and even stranger presents. The king received the deputation with great decorum and graciously accepted the presents, though he afterwards laughed at the ostriches. He soon discovered, however, that trying to keep twenty ostriches in confinement peaceably was anything but amusing, and gave them away to any of his courtiers who would accept them.

Barlow's second subject, a cassowary, was totally unknown in England until the mid-seventeenth century, when Charles II was given several of them by the directors of the East India Company. A visitor to St James's Park described one of them. He wrote, 'I saw a cassawarwa, a strange fowle somewhat lesser than an

estridge, the body about four foote high, very big in the head and like a turkey, black shining feathers or spriggs, narrow and long, which uppon him appear like soe many long haires, sleek and smooth. It hath two feathers and one quill, of which I have some to shew.' Visitors liked to pick up feathers as souvenirs of their visits to aviaries, just as we still do. In 1676 Charles rebelled at the number of cassowaries being brought to him on East India Company ships. Writing to one of his colleagues at Surat, Bombay, one of the company's scribes warned, 'His Majestie desires no more Cassawarrens'. Ostriches and cassowaries do not take kindly to confinement and are very obstreperous, especially when not given sufficient space. In their natural habitats, the ostrich roams the vast plains of Africa and the cassowary lives in dense forests in Australia and New Guinea.

Barlow painted both birds several times. He did life-size oil paintings which are now on view at Clandon House, one each side of a door in the marble hall. They are repeated in two other oil paintings at Longleat, measuring 194.5 x 133.4 cm (76.5 x 52.5 ins). He made two preliminary drawings for another picture, *Ostrich, Cassowary and Five Peacocks*, one now in the British Museum and the other in the Huntingdon Library and Art Gallery, San Marino. The original drawing was also etched by Jan Griffier the elder for *Various Birds and Beasts Drawn from the Life*, a series of plates by Barlow. It is evident that ostriches and cassowaries held special appeal for Barlow, even after the enormous labour of painting them full size twice over.

Jan van Kessel

born Antwerp 1626, died Antwerp? 1679

The Continent of America,

oil on copper, centre panel 48.5 x 67.5 cm
16 plates 14.5 x 21 cm each. Alte Pinakothek, Munich

Jan van Kessel was the son of the portrait painter Hieronymous van Kessel and his wife Paschasie, a daughter of Jan Brueghel the Elder (1568-1625). He became the pupil of his uncle Jan Brueghel the Younger (1601-1678) of Antwerp, and of Simon de Vos. In 1644 he was a master of the guild at Antwerp and married three years later. Two of his thirteen children became painters. He was a Captain of the Civic Guard in Antwerp where he worked all his life.

His output was great, both large landscapes with many kinds of living creatures, and small, exquisite studies of insects, painted in oils on tin or copper, that are delightfully accurate and well arranged. His pictures are always full of interest. He was expert at painting caterpillars and butterflies, sometimes using the lithe worms and caterpillars to form the letters and numbers of the date and his name to sign a piece of work. Some of his subjects are quite adventurous, e.g. monkeys attacking penguins, one way of bringing new species to the notice of the world. Many of his pictures were exported, for high prices, to Vienna and elsewhere during his lifetime. The Hapsburgs in particular liked his quasi-scientific paintings, hence the

1.

2.

Four of the sixteen pictures surrounding the main view of the room devoted to America. They illustrate, supposedly, the avifauna of South America. However, the penguins (1) ought to be Magellanic, but resemble jackass penguins (with haunches like those by Brueghel, see page 40). An African grey parrot (2) is perched alongside the South American macaws and birds of paradise from New Guinea. A salmon-crested cockatoo from New Guinea shares a tree branch with a scarlet macaw (3) and (4). It was many years later that correct locations were known for these birds.

3.

4.

large number of his works in the Prado. It is possible to buy his work today, one or two of his paintings are sold at auction each year.

The repetition of titles for his bird paintings shows how frequently he painted assemblies of birds — never quite the same birds, though many were repeated. His work has acquired the titles *A Concert of Birds, Allegory of Air, Chorus of Birds,* etc. The question arises, where did he find all these different bird species?

Kessel had access to cabinets of curios and did us a great service when he decided to paint the cabinets themselves, for we get a peep inside a mid-seventeenth century collector's hoard that is of immense interest for naturalists to discover what exotic species were known in Europe at that time.

Together with Erasmus Quillenius (1607-1678) Kessel painted four *Allegories of the Continents* in the form of four rooms, each one devoted to one of the then known continents, Africa, America, Asia and Europe. Each painted room was surrounded by sixteen views of cities and items from those continents showing their culture, together with the animals supposedly to be found there. In terms of painting, the completed collection of panels is a *tour de force*. In terms of geography, anthropology and natural history, they are more remarkable for their errors than anything else.

The Continent of America has been chosen because it has more small pictures that contain birds surrounding the main room than the other three continents. The American cities are nearly all South American, and eight of them are largely devoted to birds and form a weird mixture of genuinely South American species, and also species that have never been seen near that continent. The exuberance and enthusiasm with which Kessel has painted the wonders of nature and any 'curio' show that his own curiosity knew no bounds.

Kessel's bird paintings are popular because they are so colourful, with beautiful landscapes and packed with interesting species. His birds, however, do not stand close examination, because they were all painted from specimens in museum cabinets. This is soon apparent when comparing his work with that of the artists in this book who worked in menageries, or were careful to paint only those birds with which they were familiar. Kessel's birds are elongated (stretched out skins) with feathers lying incorrectly on the body (squashed corpses plumped out when set up by the taxidermist).

In his paintings of the curio cabinets this is understandable, but too often, these museums specimens have strayed outdoors and appeared in his landscapes where their live counterparts ought to be.

Jan van Kessel

Decorative Fowl and Ducklings
oils
Johnny van Haeften Gallery

This oil painting by Kessel is a beautiful landscape in some depth, where all the birds are correctly placed in their natural environment. The duck and goose families are close knit groups with the young birds exploring their surroundings. His ducklings and goslings are charming, and their beady eyes quite remarkable. Kessel shares with Bogdani (an eighteenth century Hungarian artist) a capacity either for painting beads astonishingly well, or painting eyes so round and light in colour that they obtrude with a *trompe-l'oeil* effect. Another Kessel characteristic is the slim flying birds looking anywhere but in the direction they are travelling. These are so distinctive that one hardly needs to see the signature left foreground to know instantly that this is a Jan van Kessel painting.

He has given some prominence to the purple gallinules, birds as big as a domestic chicken with deep purple-blue plumage, red legs and a very large red bill and frontal shield. It is a bird of southern Europe and parts of north Africa, so a rarity

for Kessel to paint. Shelducks and the white spoonbill were familiar in the Low Countries. Some of the long-legged brown birds, especially the one with a top-knot, and another that has caught an eel, are curiosities. Kessel sometimes let his imagination take over from reality, and it is not always possible to identify his birds.

He must have enjoyed painting this slightly larger picture as a change from the extraordinarily faithful miniaturist work on insects that he usually painted on small sheets of copper. The landscape gave Kessel the opportunity to include some delightful plants, especially the yellow waterlilies, the sedge grasses and what appear to be pinks or carnations.

All the birds appear completely relaxed, quite safe in this idyllic landscape. A sense of well-being pervades the whole scene. This is a painting full of charm and innocent activity, despite Kessel's idiosyncracies.

Johannes Spruyt

born Amsterdam 1627, died Amsterdam 1671

A Goose and Two Mallards by a Lake

oil on canvas, 73.5 x 110.5 cm
Private collection, courtesy of Rafael Valls, London

A Dutch painter, principally of live birds, after the manner of Melchior de Hondecoeter. Apart from a visit to Verona, his whole life was centred in and around Amsterdam, where he married in 1657. Of his early training nothing is known and all we have are some paintings whose colouring is bright and the drawing correct. Occasionally, he signed his work. His list of birds from which drawings were made is not extensive. He painted geese, ducks, hens, pigeons and, more rarely, a kingfisher and a ruff.

A Goose and Two Mallards by a Lake is softly lit throughout the whole of the picture, from the sky down to the clever lighting on the plumage of the birds, all combining to make this into a pleasing picture. The setting is Italianate, perhaps drawn from his memories of Verona, but more gently executed than the backgrounds of many Dutch artists who visited Italy. The larger domestic goose is seeing off a pair of mallards, the female of which has already escaped out of harm's way. The male is watching her flight as though wondering at the easy capitulation. One of the goose's goslings has already learned how to be aggressive in imitation of its parent.

Thousands of people who live in cities today have never set eyes on a live goose or duck. When Spruyt painted this picture, there can hardly have been a single person in Europe who had not seen both since most of the population lived in the country, and owned domesticated fowl. The ancestor of all domesticated geese is the greylag goose, just as all domestic ducks have descended from the mallard. This goose would weigh about ten pounds, and before providing the main ingredient for a splendid feast probably laid about one hundred eggs each year for many years. Geese are long-lived, and an English author, John Ray, in 1676 told of an eighty-year old bird. Besides providing eggs, and some down for quilts, the goose was a provider of quill pens. As late as the 1870s, a good workman could cut over twelve hundred quill pens in a day. So they were an important part of the

economy of all European countries, and Spruyt's goose would be scrutinized for its fatness and condition as well as for the pleasure of seeing a well painted familiar subject.

In England, droves of over eight hundred geese were a common sight. They were moved to fattening grounds in the Lincolnshire fens. In late September they were on the move again, walking to London this time, feeding on the commons as they went, and arrived in time for the Christmas markets. Before setting off, they were driven through hot tar and then fine grit. The resulting coatings preserved their webbed feet on the long walk.

In the eighteenth century men placed wagers on any incident with the slightest degree of unpredictability, 'Lord Orford, in 1740, made a considerable bet with the present Duke of Queensbury that a drove of Geese would beat an equal number of Turkies in a race from Norwich to London. The event proved the justice of his lordship's expectations; for the Geese kept on the road with a steady pace; but the turkies, as every evening approached, flew to roost in the trees adjoining the road, from which the drivers found it very difficult to dislodge them. In consequence of (the turkeys) stopping to sleep, the Geese beat their competitors hollow, arriving at their destination two days before the Turkies.' (Rev. W.B. Daniel, *Rural Sports*, 2 vols., 1801-13).

On 29 September 1588, Michaelmas Day, Queen Elizabeth I was supping on goose when news of the defeat of the Spanish Armada was brought to her. Thereafter, the Michaelmas Goose was eaten at this time of year in commemoration. Since Michaelmas Day was rent day for all the farmers, the landlords were often offered a present of a goose either in mitigation for part of the rent, or to keep in the landlord's good grace.

For over two hundred years after this picture was painted, viewers would see it in a very different way from that in which we see it today.

Dirck Wijntrack or Wyntrack

born Drenthe before 1625, died The Hague 1687

A Purple Heron, Ducks, Geese, Pigeons and a Swallow, in a Landscape

oil on canvas, 47.3 x 118.2 cm
Christie's London 1973, present location unknown

In his day, Wyntrack was widely recognised for his superior ability to paint birds. This particular skill was so much admired by two of the greatest Dutch landscape painters, who were his contemporaries, Jacob van Ruisdael and Johannes Wynants, that they asked him to paint the birds in their landscapes. A few barnyard scenes by Wyntrack have been preserved where the cockerels and hens are active and very well drawn and painted. Entire pictures by Wyntrack are rare, and he then shows a preference for a simple landscape, with a pool for waterfowl. The background to this picture of a purple heron with waterfowl (the birds being painted by Wyntrack) is so elaborate that it might well be the work of another artist. Without doubt, different kinds of ducks were his favourite subjects and he painted them in such a way as to make the viewer feel present by the side of the lake, watching them move with characteristic deliberation and poise, hearing them quack and splash.

The composition of this painting, with the emphasis on the left of the picture and some of the birds in the shadow of the garden balustrade with its large urn on the corner, is unusual. The plants, a thorny moss rose, frilly poppy and vine are beautifully realistically painted, and so are the snails. By contrast, a sparse distant landscape takes the eye back a great depth. The building in the middle distance is palatial, suggesting that the grounds and lake with its exotic birds, are part of a large estate. A small human figure, a horse and another (slightly overlarge) heron by the lakeside add small focal points to enliven the background. Wyntrack's water and rocks, some wet, others dry, with sunshine and shadow upon them, are exquisitely painted. He has made effective use of reflections to enhance the form of the birds. Many of his contemporaries introduced a dog, fox, cat, or a bird of prey in order to bring dramatic action into the picture, and there are several paintings by Wyntrack in which a fox creates alarm, but here all is normal interaction between the different birds. The really unusual feature in this picture, is the striking figure of the purple heron.

The purple heron looks darker and smaller than the grey heron and is a vagrant in southern and eastern England but breeds in Holland and in colonies in reed beds across the rest of Europe. Wyntrack has caught the purple heron's alert but perfectly balanced stillness and poise. The long dark streak the length of its neck is skilfully blended against the cream background. As with other birds, his painting of the feathers is beautifully soft, from the broad flight feathers to the thin filaments decorating the neck and back. Immense care has been taken to get the legs and feet correct, the position and scaliness are perfect. The same attention to detail is shown with the domestic pigeons, geese and ducks, a teal on the rock and muscovy and shoveller in the distance. To add a swallow in just that position in the sky, pointing down to all the beautiful flowers and birds which Wyntrack has painted for the sheer pleasure of texture, colour and a joy in creation, was a touch of genius.

Adriaen van Oolen

born Amsterdam c.1630, died Amsterdam 1694

Ducks and Ducklings at the Foot of a Tree in a Mediterranean Landscape

oil on canvas 89 x 76.2 cm

Private collection, Christie's Images, London

Adriaen van Oolen was the son of Jacob van Oolen, a painter, and brother of Jan. Like his brother, he painted birds in Italianate, or similar Mediterranean landscapes. His birds are native Dutch species, suggesting that he had no connections with wealthy collectors of rare birds. He concentrated on rendering every tone of the feathers in as bright a colour as nature would allow. Sometimes he took liberties with nature, as in the rather hectic turquoise of the sky and foreground water and part of the foliage. As in Jan's paintings, we are not entirely sure of the direction of the light. He, too, used the floating feather, derived from the de Hondecoeters' work, but this picture is less like a de Hondecoeter than Jan's paintings.

This picture was painted in oils on a medium size of canvas. The lapwing is flying over a domestic scene with shelducks, a hybrid duck and some indeterminate, but charming, chicks. Some bizarre cross-breeding has occurred here. The Eurasian shelduck is a large, almost goose-like duck, boldly patterned in black, white and chestnut. The drake has a red knob on his bill which the female lacks. They nest in holes in haystacks, under buildings and in old rabbit burrows. Their ducklings are white with black patches on the head and wings and down the back. But this is no ordinary pair of shelducks. The bird on the left is a strange creature whom the sheldrake must have thought to be quite beautiful, but where did she get that crest?

White crested ducks were favourite subjects with seventeenth century Dutch painters. They trace their ancestry, like all breeds of domestic ducks, back to the mallard, but we do not know how some creamy white birds with proud head carriage came to sport a large woolly-looking crest. The bird in Adriaen van Oolen's painting appears to have the curly mallard tail, a shelduck's chestnut breastband, and the white crested duck's top-knot. It proved almost impossible to breed a symmetrical crest, so that it often appeared to sit at a rakish angle on the head. The birds' owners found this most endearing, and this male sheldrake appears to have shared their taste. The chicks, however, are quite ugly ducklings and one wonders how they are going to look when in their adult plumage.

The bird that is asleep, between the two parents, is a wigeon whose striking yellowish forehead and chestnut brown head have clearly made it a suitable link for all the bright touches of orange-red in the plumage and legs of the other birds, including the flying lapwing.

Lapwings are favourite birds with artists. They grace our fields and meadowlands in considerable numbers and rid us of innumerable invertebrates, worms and insects. In spring they perform spectacular courtship flying displays and make their excited 'pee-wit' calls.

All these birds have been lovingly observed, and painted with every endeavour to get all their colours and plumage as near to nature as possible. The seventeenth century fashion for Italianate landscapes seems over-heated for these birds that we are used to seeing in cooler conditions.

Frans van Mieris
born Leiden 1635, died Leiden 1681

Lady in a Red Jacket Feeding a Parrot
oil on copper, 22.5 x 17.3 cm.
Reproduced by courtesy of the Trustees, The National Gallery, London

Several famous painters of the sixteenth and seventeenth centuries were born in Leiden, including Rembrandt, Jan Steen and Gerrit Dou. It is the seat of the oldest and most important university in Holland, founded in 1575. It was also the place to which Linnaeus went to get the first edition of his *Systema Naturae* published. The 10th edition of this work, published in 1758, is the official starting-point for zoological and botanical nomenclature, and so the basis for all scientific bird names.

Frans van Mieris was a pupil in Leyden, first as a glass-painter, then as an artist with Gerrit Dou who called him 'The Prince' of his pupils. He entered the Leiden Guild in May 1658 and served it in different official capacities. He painted pictures of poulterers' shops with many dead birds on sale, portraits and Dutch interiors. Two or three of his paintings combined a figure in an interior with a parrot, that became known as *Lady Feeding a Parrot*. A version of this theme was in Munich, now in New York, and another, *Lady in a Red Jacket Feeding a Parrot,* is in the National Gallery, London.

Frans had two sons, Willem (1662-1747) who became a successful painter, and Jan (1660-1690) whose own version of a *Lady Feeding a Parrot* is currently in the Dowes Fine Art Gallery, London. Jan was so anxious to emulate his father and achieve his standards, that he overworked, became ill and his illness led to his early death. Jan's African grey parrot is small, and a minor element in his interior scene where a number of figures are of primary importance. In Frans van Mieris' *Lady in a Red Jacket Feeding a Parrot* the bird is nearly of equal importance with its mistress.

Frans van Mieris' painting once belonged to Sir Robert Peel, British Prime Minister in 1834 and 1841-46, who bought it in 1823 for 305 guineas (£320.5s.). When harassed by the problems of government, he said that he liked the feeling of tranquillity that this picture gave to him. The National Gallery acquired it in 1871.

If the very first 'parrot' known in Europe was really a parakeet with long tail (see Van Eyck, page 14), the African grey was probably the first parrot to be brought to Europe. The word 'parrot' was first used in England c.1525, for what had until that time been called a popinjay. The African grey was painted by Lucas Cranach c.1520 in his *Adam and Eve in Paradise*, and other pictures by him. It was frequently used to provide the bright spot of red that we have seen was so much valued to enliven forest scenes or dark interiors. In order to show the red undertail, this parrot is often drawn in a tipped position, head down beneath the level of its feet on a perch. This is quite a natural posture, as it happens, and very convenient for artists.

The African grey parrot is one of the best mimics of the human voice. It was accorded special status by the church for whom it became a symbol of eloquence. Then it was observed that the density of feathers kept the parrot dry in heavy rain, and so it became a symbol of virginal purity. Parrots preen one another's feathers, in what appears to be a show of affection, so they next acquired the symbolic meaning of Christian love. These meanings were apparent in the sixteenth and

seventeenth centuries, but when paintings ceased to be closely connected to religion, the parrot retained only the symbolic meaning of love. The presence of a parrot in a picture of this period, when Frans van Mieris was painting his ladies feeding their parrots, denoted love between men and women.

Another change had taken place. Whereas the ownership of a parrot had once signified great wealth, now parrots were pet birds in many households, and appear in Dutch interior scenes of quite modest homes. Presents of parrots were made by many Dutch and Flemish men to their ladies, as tokens of love, and when we see pictures of the ladies taking such an interest in their birds and feeding them, we know that these tokens were highly regarded and cherished as being very special pets.

The African grey in this picture has its own piece of furniture, a parrot stand. It is noticeable that, from the very earliest representations of parrots in art, on Greek mosaics or Roman frescoes, in fifteenth century easel paintings onwards, all the parrots are shown freely moving about rooms or walking along balustrades. Unlike other pet birds, they are not confined to cages. When paintings of Dutch interiors became popular, a parrot was frequently included, and nearly as often, a parrot stand. It would be interesting to know who first devised this ornamental tree.

Melchior de Hondecoeter
born Utrecht 1636, died Amsterdam 1695

Birds by a Pool
oil on canvas, 153.5 x 186.2cm
Signed 'M. d Hondecoeter'. Christie's Images

Melchior was the grandson of the landscape painter Gillis de Hondecoeter and the son and pupil of Gysbert de Hondecoeter. After the death of his father, when he was about seventeen, he went as pupil to his uncle Jan Baptist Weenix (1621-1663) who had spent the years 1642-46 in Italy. He owed the idea of using decorative Italianate landscapes and buildings or ruins to his uncle's influence. From Weenix he also learned the patient observation of detail that later helped to make his own paintings so true to life.

Melchior de Hondecoeter was at The Hague by 1659 but went to settle in Amsterdam in 1663 where he remained for the rest of his life and died on 3 April 1695. His earliest paintings, dated from 1668, including the one in the National Gallery, London, were based on the style of Otto Marseus van Schrieck (1619/20-1678) who had many imitators about that period.

The range of subjects of his paintings was quite small, all based on wildfowl, poultry and exotic bird species in landscapes, ornamental gardens and farmyard

1. White pelican 2. Sheldrake 3. Cassowary 4. Greater flamingo 5. Salmon-crested cockatoo
6. Crowned crane 7. Great curassow 8. Guinea fowl 9. Egyptian goose 10. Muscovy goose
11. Wigeon 12. Red-breasted goose 13. Goosander 14. Chough 15. Turkey

Feathers are mainly of two types, down and contour feathers. On full grown birds, an underlying down keeps them warm, while the outward shape of the bird is formed by the contour feathers. Most contour feathers have a downy lower section, like the one de Hondecoeter has painted here. The number of feathers on a bird varies from under 1,000 on a hummingbird to about 25,000 on a swan in winter.

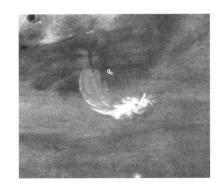

settings. He had such facility that he could catch the movements of birds in full action. In order to paint them accurately from life, he bred large numbers of them in his garden. His lively paintings were achieved by introducing an eagle attacking from the sky, or turkeys and cocks fighting. Either way, the birds are swiftly avoiding being caught, small chicks which cannot get out of the way in time are sent sprawling, and feathers fly.

The floating feather, and feathers on the ground, became a hallmark of Melchior de Hondecoeter's work and are as meticulously painted as those still attached to the birds. The feeling of movement was assisted by one of de Hondecoeter's artistic innovations. He painted only part of a bird at the edge of his canvas, so that they are seen to be departing from, or just arriving on, the scene. This adds to the impression that the viewer has just chanced on a delightful garden full of birds and is, himself, a part of it.

This particular picture of *Birds by a Pool* is very similar to *Pelican and Other Birds Near a Pool*, which has the sub-title, *The Floating Feather*, c.1680, oil on canvas, 159 x 144cm, which is in the Rijksmuseum, Amsterdam. De Hondecoeter has skilfully arranged the birds so as to show their main diagnostic features, each being accurately portrayed in character and relative size. Dramatic foreground lighting is used to contrast with the dark trees and clouds.

The number and range of unusual species is notable, the white pelican taking pride of place in the foreground. The white pelican lives in eastern Europe and de Hondecoeter would probably have painted it in a menagerie. This particular bird is in its finest breeding plumage when there is a rosy tint to the white feathers and a short shaggy crest on the back of the head. Its size is emphasized by the group of ducks nearby and the large birds in the mid-ground. The tall cassowary, greater flamingo and crowned crane are correctly painted in relation to the foreground pelican and also to the distant flamingo and crane.

De Hondecoeter has also collected some geese that had been introduced into Europe and bred successfully in the protection of ornamental gardens and aviaries. In the wild, the handsome red-breasted goose breeds on the Siberian tundra, and the Egyptian goose, as its name implies, breeds naturally in Egypt from Lake Nasser southwards, wintering along the Nile. Muscovy ducks were first introduced by the Spaniards from Cartagena in Colombia, South America in the sixteenth century, and two authors cataloguing all known bird species in 1555 reported that these newly introduced ducks had bred so well that they were sold on the open market. As usual, some common species, selected for their beautiful colours and plumage markings, are also included in the picture. The bay-breasted shelduck is a very handsome bird, and the wigeon with its cinnamon colouring and fine vermiculation on its back, would be a far more familiar species in Holland. There is still space in this totally unnatural but very natural-seeming assembly of birds for a merganser and the chough, a guinea fowl and black curassow. In the Rijksmuseum version, the chough is replaced by a smew, a pintail occupies the position of the shelduck, and a teal appears between the pelican and merganser. There is also a brent goose and the muscovy is just appearing on the scene, rather than painted in full as in this version. In the distance a crowned crane in this picture has replaced a splendid sarus crane. The greatest difference, however, is the appearance of a branch jutting out from the trees on the left on which a salmon-crested cockatoo is perched. The large stone arch is another addition in this version.

Such pictures must have given their owners endless pleasure in looking for the different species, remembering when they saw them in the menagerie, and enjoying the sheer skill of the artist in recording them so realistically.

Melchior de Hondecoeter

A Concert of Birds
oil on canvas, 138 x 174 cm. Courtesy Richard Green Gallery

In the course of his thirty-five years as a painter, Melchior de Hondecoeter inevitably repeated the same themes several times. However, unlike Brueghel who painted the *Garden of Eden* and placed each animal in the same position and with very little variation in the landscape, de Hondecoeter varied his scenes and the collection of birds. Finding a new de Hondecoeter always creates a feeling of happy anticipation as one wonders which new species he has chosen this time. Has he used an Italianate landscape with ruins, a courtyard, a park, some different architectural features, or, as in this *A Concert of Birds*, a simple woodland scene with a small distant view? Occasionally there is a detail that he has not used elsewhere, such as his signature in an unusual place, as on this music manuscript book. Were these his spectacles, with no side-pieces? By the mid-seventeenth century most spectacles had side-pieces and a scale of lens strengths had been worked out proportionate to the number of years a man was past middle age (the prescription being double the strength of lens for a woman of the same age owing to her 'inherent feminine weakness'). These lenses do little to enlarge the music and there is not the slightest evidence of any visual defect in Melchior de Hondecoeter's work. Perhaps they are put there in reference to a Dutch proverb: "What is the use

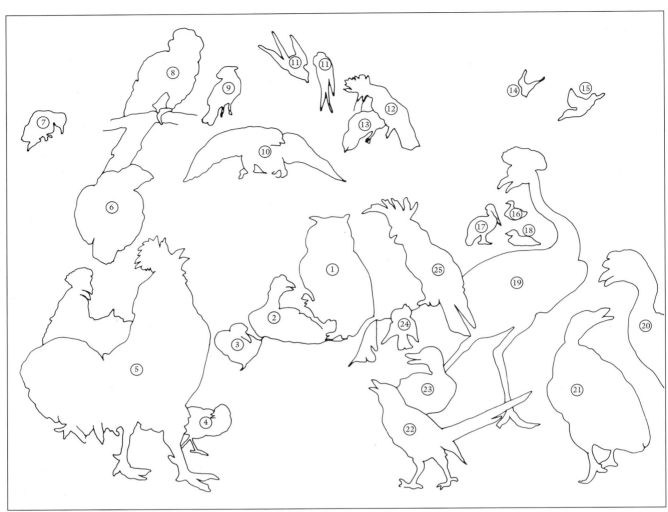

1. Short-eared owl 2. Black francolin 3. Lapwing 4. Siberian jay 5. Domestic cock 6. Blue-fronted amazon 7. Great spotted woodpecker 8. Scarlet macaw 9. Waxwing 10. Kestrel 11. Swallows 12. Hoopoe 13. Pigeon 14. Swallow? 15. Kingfisher 16. Mute swan 17. Pelican 18. Muscovy duck 19. Crowned crane 20. Black curassow 21. Sheldrake 22. Magpie 23. Wigeon 24. Great titmouse 25. Sulphur-crested cockatoo

of a candle and glasses if the owl does not want to see".

His detail is extraordinarily good, from the slight pink on the back of the pelican next to the muscovy duck in the background to the tiny light feathers over the beak of the Siberian jay appearing round the legs of the chief cockerel chorister.

Most of the birds are singing, but perhaps the swans, being mute, are deliberately placed too far away to join in. A kingfisher and swallow are about to join the other birds, and the black curassow has only just arrived on the scene and is being given his cue by the sheldrake. The magpie, wigeon, lapwing and black francolin, with a precariously balanced great titmouse, are singing lustily in time to the conducting of the short-eared owl choirmaster.

One doubts the tunefulness of the sulphur-crested cockatoo and blue-fronted amazon, or the crowned crane. The great spotted woodpecker is singing rather than drumming. The scarlet macaw appears slightly bored and the waxwing has turned his back on the proceedings, but the swallows are twittering excitedly. The hoopoe, like some human choristers, looks comical with its mouth wide open, but it may be difficult for a hoopoe to reach the top notes. He is evidently one of the descants. A pigeon and kestrel are struggling hard to hold this manuscript part still, as it blows in a breeze.

One curious feature of all paintings of bird concerts, by different artists, is the total lack of consideration of the vocal qualities of the birds they include. The choice and positioning of the birds is purely aesthetic, bearing no relation to whether they sing or quack, whistle or croak. There is no gathering together of such wonderful songsters as the nightingale and wood lark, song-thrush and blackbird, for example. An artist taking this theme today would probably depict the birds at a dawn chorus. In the seventeenth century, there was not as yet an understanding of why birds sing, or a full appreciation of this timing of the spring outpouring of bird music.

However amusing his concept of a bird concert, de Hondecoeter has used the theme to paint a very remarkable gathering of birds, each one beautifully realistic and gloriously faithfully coloured. Every detail is superbly observed, from the fence and tree stump to the small loose feathers. This is a truly magnificent, large painting that could be viewed time and again, and still some small, new, detail would give pleasure. This is the quality that marks a truly great painting, and de Hondecoeter repeatedly produced bird paintings to this standard.

Melchior de Hondecoeter

A Classical Garden Landscape With Golden Eagle and Other Birds

oil on canvas
184.2 x 125.7 cm. Rafael Valls, London

Melchior de Hondecoeter's output was large, and his work in constant demand. He had many imitators who worked in his style and copied his compositions well into the next century. He is the best known, and the most skilled, of the Dutch/Flemish bird painters, acknowledged both in his own lifetime and subsequently to be the master of Dutch bird painting. His work is in many European museums.

He painted panels for country houses and palaces, often designed to fit certain positions. A decorative piece for the palace of Soestdijk which Prince William III bought and had rebuilt, included a large urn with cockatoos, other parrots and monkeys from the Prince's menagerie in the gardens. A garden terrace, with an urn, a distant view of the landscape beyond the garden, and some trees, were ideal settings for de Hondecoeter's birds. Some of his paintings were very large, including full-sized birds from peacocks down to small species, but always in the correct proportions one to another. These grandiose pieces appealed to collectors with large houses whose walls they decorated. The classical features in the pictures aided de Hondecoeter's structural composition and had the added advantage that they intimated that the owner of the picture was a man of culture.

A Classical Garden Landscape is a large canvas allowing de Hondecoeter to work on a grand scale. He has painted a garden on a warm summer evening with roses in full bloom, the fountain cascading and a large tree to provide cool shade for the birds on the balustrade. A golden eagle has burst onto this idyllic scene, causing alarm and scattering the ducks in several directions. A garganey is safe high above the garden, but the turnstone, the bird nearest the eagle, is flying fast in order to escape. Also caught in the air are a pintail and a teal near the fountain, and a shoveller has already almost departed from the scene. On the balustrade the shelduck, with its back to the eagle, has not yet perceived any danger, but the young brent goose is newly aware of it, and a wigeon is losing no time in diving off the ledge. The shoveller seems unaware, for it, too, has its back to the eagle, but the goosander is clearly alarmed and about to take evasive action. All the drakes in this picture are readily identifiable, in correct size in relation to one another, and appear in the right posture, just as a bird-watcher would hope to see them under these circumstances. The floating feather at the bottom of the picture adds a small touch of poignancy, for we do not really believe the eagle can make a kill in such an idyllic place, but the feather reminds us of the fragility and vulnerability of birds.

The golden eagle has been so positioned as to catch the sun's rays on the back, head and neck feathers. The bird is much darker than suggested here, but artistic licence is invariably taken by all painters who find this wonderful bird of prey an irresistible subject. De Hondecoeter has hidden the tip of one wing behind the tree, adding to the impression that the eagle has just this moment appeared. Its talons may be curled under, but are menacingly visible nonetheless. This is a remarkably good picture of the eagle, and the other birds, in flight.

Frans van Cuyck, or Myerop

born Bruges 1640 or 22 November 1662, died Ghent c.1690

Still Life With Bittern

oil on canvas, 119 x 92.5 cm, signed
Groeningemuseum, Bruges

Very little is known about this Flemish painter whose date of birth, even, is still in doubt. He was a painter of portraits as well as still life. Among his still lifes is one of the most impressive illusionist bird pictures ever painted.

This picture hangs in a small gallery in the Groeningemuseum, Bruges, where it literally stops the visitor in his tracks. Many pictures in a gallery earn but a cursory glance, or a short pause, as visitors walk through. This one demands full attention, and invariably receives it.

The main bird is a bittern but the other two smaller ones are not so easy to recognise. They are probably a small dark song-bird and one of the long-billed waders. All the birds appear, at first glance, to be present in the flesh, hung against the plain white background around which there is a black frame. The stunning impact is achieved, not only by the completely realistic painting of the feathers, but by the deep shadows painted on the right hand side of the birds, indicating a light source from the left. To add to the illusion, Cuyck painted a black border round the edge of the picture that looks like part of the frame, and then over-lapped it with one wing-tip. Only the narrow outer black line is the real frame.

This kind of illusionist painting is called *trompe-l'oeil*, a deception of the eye. Standing back from the painting the viewer is convinced he can see a dead bird hanging from the nail, and moves forward to take a closer look. When a gallery visitor has already seen a number of *trompe-l'oeils*, he is not so easily deceived, but one can readily understand the amazement of a first-time viewer, and imagine the astonishment that greeted the very first *trompe-l'oeil* deception ever perpetrated. The earliest *trompe-l'oeil* is attributed to an ancient Greek painter called Zeuxis, who worked at the end of the fifth century B.C. and specialised in panel pictures (rather than the usual wall paintings of the time). He painted such realistic grapes that birds came to peck at them, mistaking them for genuine fruit. Optical illusions like this have been popular whenever an artist has indulged in this kind of painting. One of the first bird *trompe-l'oeils* was by the Venetian artist Jacopo de 'Barbari, whose *Still Life With Partridge, Mail Gloves and Bolt from a Crossbow* was mentioned on page 9.

The subject of this painting is a bittern whose plumage is buff, pale and darker brown with black, arrow-head markings. This is a life-size painting of the bittern that is 70 to 80 centimetres in length and has a wing span of 125 to 135 centimetres. In order for a *trompe-l'oeil* to truly deceive, the object has to be perfectly accurately painted both in colour, shape and texture. Cuyck has achieved this, from the claws and skin of the legs, through the beautiful feathers to the sharp bill.

D. D. E. VANDERSTOELE 1890

119

Johannes Bronckhorst
born Leyden 1648, died Hoorn 1726

An Assembly of Exotic Birds in a Landscape
oil on canvas, 55 x 73 cm
Private collection, courtesy of Rafael Valls, London

Bronckhorst was first employed as a pastry-cook, but abandoned that career from the time he settled in Hoorn in 1670. Hoorn was then one of the chief sea ports of Holland, being especially active in herring fishing until the Zuider Zee silted up at the end of the seventeenth century. In its heyday, it was the principal town of West Friesland, whose most famous native was Willem Schouten (1580-1625) who rounded the southern cape of the Americas on two occasions, naming it Cape Hoorn (now Horn). The sea port probably attracted Bronckhorst as the place where exotics from the west and east Indies were brought ashore.

In Hoorn, Bronckhorst painted the most careful, beautifully coloured pictures of insects, flowers and birds, using watercolours and gouache on vellum. Sometimes he made simple studies of single species, but more often he placed his birds in pleasant open country landscapes that never detracted from the birds in the foreground. All his compositions were finely drawn.

Bronckhorst was more interested in making a faithful record of a few exotic birds than de Hondecoeter and van Oolen, who liked a lot of birds in their canvases, mixing exotics with farmyard birds. Bronckhorst carefully spaced his birds, all of

1. Great curassow female 2. Scarlet macaw 3. Silver pheasant 4. Golden pheasant
5. and 6. Greater flamingo 7. Blue-crowned pigeon

them rare, to show them in all their beauty, with no distractions such as quarrelling cockerels. Each one of his birds deserves our full attention, those in the background as much as the nearer birds.

An Assembly of Exotic Birds in a Landscape has several exotics. The blue-crowned pigeon is about the size of a large domestic chicken and as heavily built, with stout legs. Its crown is a large, laterally-compressed crest of lacy feathers that are a delicate blue-grey with a silvery tinge. Most of its plumage is a medium blue but the upper part of the mantle and most of the wing coverts are dark purplish-red. Bronckhorst's colouring, shape and size are quite correct, but it is a pity that the very pretty crest is lost against the background.

The red macaw, golden pheasant (with red breast) and red-legged and red-faced silver pheasant form a deliberate triangle of bright reds. Exotic pheasants have long been popular aviary birds owing to their brilliant plumage colours and spectacularly long tails. Like the crest of the blue-crowned pigeon, the tails of these two pheasants are laterally-compressed. The first record of the golden pheasant in captivity in England was made by Eleazar Albin in 1740, so this painting predates that by nearly a century.

The gold feathering is found on the back, the head, and as a deeper shade on the ruff. The male golden pheasant, when displaying to a female, spreads the ruff widely and lowers his wing to reveal his golden back, so that he is truly called a golden pheasant, despite the amount of brilliant crimson in his plumage.

The silver pheasant is not so popular and when first introduced into England in 1740 was often called a pencilled pheasant. It is white on the back and tail where the black, wavy pencil lines are clearly visible in Bronckhorst's painting. The blue-black of the crest and under plumage is an intense colour, and so is the bright red of the face wattles. This species lives in China, Burma, Thailand, Vietnam, Laos and Cambodia, while the golden pheasant is confined, in the wild, to China.

The female great curassow on the left is watching the displaying male flamingo, while the other flamingo also regards his downward pointing beak and raised wings with polite interest. One of his pink feathers has been shaken out during his excited flapping. The greater flamingo is an inhabitant of southern Spain and France, feeding in shallow saline lakes. It immerses its head, turns the bill upside down and with a scything motion sucks in the water which it then filters through its bill to extract small invertebrates and plankton. One of the most picturesque and beautiful of the world's birds, it is also among the tallest (125-145 cm) and flies fully extended, neck stretched out in front, legs behind. It builds remarkable mud-pie nests called vetones, on which the downy grey chicks sit like small kings in their castles. It was not until 1837, when Edward Lear painted a picture of a flamingo sitting on its nest, that this normal manner of incubation was illustrated. Until then, the flamingo had been thought to straddle its eggs while still standing. Since its legs and neck are longer in proportion to the body than any other bird, no-one could imagine how it could fold its legs in order to sit down.

The curassow is a large turkey-like South American bird that was thought to have come from the island of Curaçao in the Dutch West Indies, hence its name. Spanish-speaking south and central Americans call them *pavo del monte*, mountain peacocks. These gentle, curly-crested birds belong to the same family as turkeys, and their meat is like a richer more flavoursome turkey.

Maria Sibylla Merian

born Frankfurt am Main 1647, died Amsterdam 1717
The Lapwing
watercolour with gum arabic varnishing on vellum
31 x 25.5cm, Department of Drawing, Harvard University Art Museums,
Harvard University, Cambridge, Massachusetts

Maria Merian is the first notable woman to paint natural history subjects. She was born into a family of engravers and her father, Matthaeus Merian, was an etcher and book publisher. When he died, her mother married Jacob Marrell, a German painter who specialised in flower pieces. He recognised Maria's talent and was both her art teacher and, perhaps more importantly, took her on field trips to observe nature for herself. Maria married one of Marrell's pupils, Johann Andreas Graff in 1665 and had two daughters, but the marriage ended in divorce c.1693. She joined a sect called the Labadists who had several missions in Surinam (Dutch Guiana). Maria took her artistic daughter Dorothea to Surinam, 1699-1701, in order to study the insects, flowers and birds, all of which she painted in watercolours. Her brushwork is dense and her colours fresh and clean. Goethe remarked on her style, saying that it moved 'to and fro between art and science, between observation of nature and painterly aims.'

The lapwing is one of the most graceful birds in the European countryside. Maria Merian has caught the grace of this species, even though she is working from a mounted model. She has managed to make the bird look alive, but two features in particular give away the fact that she worked from a stuffed bird. The first is the feet – birds are not in the habit of treading on their own toes, the second is the head turned back over the body. This is a taxidermist's ploy, seen repeatedly in their models ever since taxidermy was first practised in the seventeenth century. If the bill were to face the correct way, the model would take up more space in a glass case or on a shelf. Furthermore, a careless handler might catch the bill and tear the head from the neck. Hundreds of bird illustrations in books, first painted and then engraved or lithographed using mounted models, are shown in this unnatural position, the result of taxidermists' practicality.

Despite this, Maria's lapwing is a beautiful study and a truly delightful painting of this familiar, yet overlooked species. In the air, it is a black and white bird with rounded wings and a flight pattern that has earned it the nickname 'flopwing'. It has many other nicknames, including 'peewit' which is derived from its call. This is heard in spring when the male birds perform aerial acrobatics, calling excitedly, to which a loud humming sound is added from the wings. It moves to coastal pastures in winter, particularly if the weather is harsh, so that its call carrying across inland fields in March is an early sign of spring.

Where there are many lapwings in a field, close to the road verge, it is always a pleasure to stop and take the opportunity to look more closely at these surprisingly colourful birds. The distant black and white pattern suddenly takes on wonderful iridescent green and bronze hues on the back, while a chestnut patch on the wing is subtly echoed by the under tail coverts. The long wispy crest makes it unique among waders, and to see this blowing uncontrollably in the wind evokes the idea of a marsh sprite. Despite being a substantial bird, it always seems particularly light and buoyant.

Maria Merian's painting of the lapwing is clearly a work inspired by field memories of this elegant master of aerobatics.

David Klöcker Ehrenstrahl
born Hamburg 1629, died Stockholm 1698

Blackcocks in Springtime
oil on canvas, dated 1675. Nationalmuseum, Stockholm

Ehrenstrahl was a talented German bird artist whose paintings are preserved in Stockholm where he spent much of his working life. He is regarded as being primarily a portrait painter having executed a number of portraits of the Swedish royal family and aristocracy. He learned the basics of his art from Juriaen Jacobszoon in 1648 at Amsterdam and then went to Rome to work with Pietro da Cortona. Three years later he visited Sweden, then returned to Germany and Italy. He went to Sweden in 1651 and was appointed court painter there ten years later. So much of his work was done in Sweden, that he may almost be regarded as a Swedish painter. He certainly appreciated the beautiful Swedish landscapes of lakes and forest, and painted them evocatively.

Ehrenstrahl was attracted to black grouse, or black game as sportsmen call them, and painted them more than once. A remarkably fine illusionist oil painting of two blackcocks suspended against a wooden panel, with exquisitely painted plumage is now at the Nationalmuseum, Stockholm. *Blackcocks in Springtime* is a most unusual painting, not just for its period, 1675, but for any time. Ehrenstrahl has painted a lek in progress, with lively birds in full action, on the lekking ground in a correct environment with a delightful landscape background. He must have got up before dawn, gone to the edge of the forest and observed the birds for some time in order to achieve this record of *Blackcocks in Springtime*.

A blackcock is the size of a large rooster, with glossy blue-black plumage except for a narrow white wing bar and white undertail coverts. The lyre-shaped outer tail feathers are its most distinguished feature. The female is called a grey hen owing to her much duller appearance, being brownish in colour barred with black, and she is five inches shorter than the male. Her inconspicuous colouring is advantageous while she broods and rears the chicks.

In spring the blackcocks emerge at dawn from the mixed woodland and brushland where they roost, to gather in groups on flat ground in clearings or on adjoining moorland, bogs or pastures, where each cock establishes a small territory for display purposes. The lekking ground soon becomes a noisy battleground with the males bowing and scraping with spread tails, wings half opened and the red wattles above their eyes distended. This display is aimed at attracting females drawn to the scene by crowing noises and a bubbling, surprisingly musical, cooing. Where males meet on the boundaries of their territories furious battles appear to ensue, though it is all bluff and noise. The females wait in the trees and on the edges of the lek, stand around or peck the ground in apparent indifference, but are really keenly observant for it is they who select the males with whom they are prepared to mate. Shortly after sunrise, the birds fly up into the trees, and the excitement is over for that day.

Ehrenstrahl has recorded all these facts, but in such a lively and convincing manner, and with such skill in depicting the foreground, mid and background features of the landscape, that it is both an ornithologically satisfying painting, and an artistic composition. This is a rare achievement, and one which our present-day artists would admire.

Jan van Oolen
born 1651, died 1698

A Brace of Mallard, a White Goose, a Curlew, a Snipe and Other Birds by a Plinth With a Coastal Landscape
oil on canvas, 110 x 134.7cm
Private collection, courtesy of Rafael Valls, London

Jan van Oolen was a Dutch painter of birds, landscape, still life and game. He specialised in painting compositions of exotic birds in landscape settings, that were usually large and signed. His signed works are rare today because his signature has been removed in order to attribute his work to Melchior de Hondecoeter. This situation is further confused where he deliberately imitated and copied the works of Melchior de Hondecoeter (including a floating feather) with such success that they pass for originals. He may also be confused with Dirck Wyntrack as they have a similar colour scheme. He was born and died in Amsterdam, the son of the painter Jacob van Oolen and brother of Adriaen. When he worked on his own, original compositions, he was only slightly inferior to Melchior de Hondecoeter, which is another reason why his canvases are often hung in galleries under the name of de Hondecoeter. He had less delicacy and his colours were harsher and less glowing than those of the great master.

This painting shows similar coarse-leaved foliage as that in the painting by Adriaen, but the picture is enhanced by the inclusion of wild flowers. Another similarity lies in the intense blue of the sky and the golden cloud linings. Jan's birds are disturbed by a couple of people who have just come round the corner by the seashore. As the light falls on the head of the alarmed male mallard, Oolen has tried to capture the iridescent green. Depending on the light, a mallard's head is seen as black, dark green or a beautiful iridescent green. It is not surprising that mallards feature so often in paintings. They domesticate very easily and lose their wild characteristics when in captivity. Unfortunately, these include their sleek lines, long necks and perfectly proportioned heads, for they become fatter in the body, shorter in the neck and heavier in the head. However, they retain the attractive and unique curl of feathers in the tail.

The downward curve of the curlew's beak is accentuated by its being open and so we see two sweeping curves of both mandibles, but no tongue. One can almost hear the curlew's cry of alarm. In another moment it will have become long and sleek, facing to the left, ready for flight. The curlew rarely appears in early paintings, though there is an example of a flying curlew in Tintoretto's *Creation of the Birds and the Fishes*, 1550-53.

The snipe, looking at the curlew, is also raising its wings, rather for the benefit of the artist than to meet any exigencies of the situation, for it will not take off while looking over its shoulder. Both curlew and snipe are marsh birds and may have been seen by this inlet, but the group, as in so many paintings of this period, is artificial.

The collection of assorted birds in a landscape, a feature of Dutch and Flemish painting in the seventeenth and eighteenth centuries in particular, reminds one of the manner in which other artists of the same period assembled their huge flower pieces. The exotic blooms, imported from all the colonies, with flowers gathered from Dutch gardens at all seasons, were carefully painted into the bouquet, as and when they became available. The gorgeous flower pictures were painted over a long period, sometimes a year or longer. Bird artists working in aviaries to record exotic foreign species may also have waited for new arrivals when working to commission for a collector. They also had many native bird species that could easily be seen in spring by walking along the dykes, such as the curlew and snipe in this picture. Domestic birds were to hand, which is why this white goose (whose feathers are beautifully painted) is included with the mallards. The de Hondecoeters assembled foreign, native and domesticated birds in one painting. They, with Oolen and other bird artists, would also be brought unusual captured and injured birds for them to include in their pictures, which they painted over a period of time. This method of working did not make it easy to compose an harmonious picture, though it was probably easier with flowers than with birds. The blue-backed bird with speckled breast, which is flying in from the right, certainly appears to have been an after-thought.

This is a picture to be enjoyed for its colour, scenery, and very skilled painting of the birds' feathers, particularly the speckled plumage. It is more pleasing artistically, than ornithologically, which is why van Oolen cannot be rated as highly as Melchior de Hondecoeter.

Franz de Hamilton
fl. 1661-1695

Concert of Birds

oil on copper, 61.8 x 77.4 cm. Staatliche Kunsthalle, Karlsruhe

This lively *Concert of Birds* is not a typical painting by Franz de Hamilton, but it was one of his most inspired pictures. Usually, he was a painter of historical subjects, and still life studies of plants and flowers into which he introduced some live reptiles and insects. He also painted dead birds.

Hamilton is an obscure artist about whom little is known. The first piece of evidence is a record of him, in 1661, at Cleves in the service of the Elector of Brandenburg who took him to Potsdam where he remained until 1671. After a visit to Vienna 1672-74, he became attached to the court of the Landgrave of Hesse-Cassel from 1675, in Hanover, and was active in southern Germany as a Bavarian court painter from 1683 to 1689 for Elector Maximilian II. He continued to move around the different provinces that were destined to be joined together to become Prussia in 1701. He was also in Munich and Augsburg, but his place and date of death are not known.

This *Concert of Birds* is now in the Staatliche Kunsthalle, Karlsruhe, where it had been thought to be by Jan van Kessel until post-war research prompted a closer inspection of the painting and revealed a signature in the bottom right hand corner

1. Ostrich 2. Black stork 3. Crowned crane 4. Pelican 5. Cormorant 6. Peacock 7. Lapwing 8. Rock partridge 9. Bean goose 10. Chinese goose 11. Cassowary 12. Crane 13. Goldfinch 14. Chattering lory 15. Blue titmouse 16. Woodchat shrike 17. Blue and gold macaw 18. Blackbird 19. Buzzard 20. Grey shrike 21. Amazon parrot sp. 22. Brambling 23. Jay 24. Salmon-crested cockatoo 25. Fieldfare 26. Toucan sp. 27. Redwing 28. Great titmouse 29. Chaffinch 30. Mistlethrush 31. Bullfinch 32. Golden eagle juvenile 33. Hawfinch 34. Cuckoo 35. Red-faced lovebird 36. Long-eared owl 37. Hobby 38. Wood pigeon 39. Red-footed falcon 40. Honey buzzard? 41. Linnet 42. Roller 43. Magpie 44. Scarlet macaw 45. Bearded reedling 46. Waxwing 47. Little owls 48. Hoopoe 49. Wren 50. Pheasant 51. Red-breasted merganser 52. Bustard 53. Whooper swan 54. Mute swan 55. Shoveller 56. Egyptian goose 57. Purple heron juvenile 58. Heron 59. White stork 60. Mallard 61. Goosanders 62. Kingfisher

'F.D.H.'. It has subsequently been traced back to the collection of the Margrave of Baden-Baden at Schloss Rastatt (near Baden-Baden) where it was listed in an inventory of 1772 as a large painting, on copper, 'no. 8 by Hamilton'.

This kind of painstaking research of seventeenth century and earlier paintings is often necessary due to the extensive amount of copying of earlier masters, the repetition of the same subject matter (such as bird concerts and gardens of paradise as we have already seen), and the lack of signatures on many paintings. There has been a good deal more cleaning of pictures in recent years, when some canvases have been taken out of their frames for the first time since they were painted. The revelation of a signature, sometimes also a date, has meant several paintings, for-

Athanasius Kircher's musical notation for the song of the nightingale in his transnotation of bird voices published in 1650. Below are the cockerel's and hen's calls, two notes of the cuckoo, the quail's trisyllabic song and macaw's squawk

merly wrongly attributed, are now being re-attributed. That the birds in this painting by Hamilton are superior to those painted by Kessel would be obvious were the two artists' bird pictures to be placed side by side. When an exhibition of paintings collects a number together, it is easier to compare them and mistakes in attribution can then be put right. It still requires a person with a knowledge of both art and ornithology, but with the recent concern for our wildlife and a greater interest in bird art, such people are becoming more numerous.

Hamilton's *Concert of Birds* was a theme used by several artists. Kessel, Melchior de Hondecoeter and Savery, to name but three artists, each painted several with this title. It provided a wonderful opportunity to paint a large number of birds, in and around a tree, all there for the purpose of singing. In the mid-seventeenth century, they were just beginning to take an interest in bird songs and to transcribe them into musical notation. Athanasius Kircher, in 1650, was one of the first musicians to publish a book on this aspect of bird life. Nearly all the pictures of bird choirs include an owl (or eagle here) in charge of the music, sometimes with a leg raised as though conducting. Close scrutiny of the music occasionally reveals the text from some musician's ideas of musical notation for bird songs.

Members of this choir include an ostrich, crowned crane, pelican, cormorant, peacock, lapwing, partridge, bustard, pheasants, swans, heron, ducks and geese, macaws and other parrots, magpie, the eagle conductor, hoopoe, owl, sparrowhawk, cassowary and another crane. Less usual species in bird pictures are the swan goose, more familiarly known as a Chinese goose in its domesticated form, and the black stork of eastern Europe. It is obvious the soloists are going to have to be the great tit and chaffinch, aided by some of the small birds in the top branches – if they can make themselves heard above the cacophony from the ground.

Christoph Ludwig Agricola

born Ratisbone 1667, died Regensburg 1719

Crossbill

watercolour. Courtesy of Rafael Valls, London

This German artist painted on the grand scale when working on landscapes or pictures with architectural features, but could scale down to detailed water-colour painting of flowers, butterflies and birds that were of great merit as nature studies. He was also an engraver, a fact that is self-evident in the way he drew and coloured his bird studies.

Like Maria Merian, Agricola spans the seventeenth/eighteenth century, and their work incorporates elements of painstaking truthfulness to nature in colouring and texture, dating back to Dürer, and a growing awareness of the need for scientific accuracy that would play an increasing role in the course of the eighteenth century. If Maria Merian's work went 'to and fro between art and science', Agricola's was more firmly on the side of science and was influenced also by the needs of the engraver.

Artists who prepared drawings for the engraver and etcher to copy were expected to supply a line drawing with every mark that the burin or etching needle would copy. Each contour was outlined and then filled in with minute lines to represent the feathers, also the scales on the legs. In addition, any shading and variations in depth of colour were indicated. Nevertheless, however relaxed and life-like the original watercolour painting, a certain stiffness was inevitably introduced at the engraving stage, because it was difficult to produce a flowing line with a burin gouging a line through copper. This is why early eighteenth century bird book illustrations are so unnaturally stiff. As a result, a gap opened up between bird painting and bird illustration. The first could be vitally alive and full of action with well-proportioned birds and beautiful colouring, while the second frequently showed the birds ill-drawn, wrongly proportioned and, because cheaper pigments were often used for colouring books, also badly coloured. It is unlikely that an engraving of Agricola's crossbill would have looked as good a picture of the bird as this watercolour.

Crossbills are remarkable birds for their colouring, their strange beaks and their irregular appearance in large flocks where they are not normally resident. Agricola has painted a male crossbill and achieved a close approximation to its orange-red or brick red feathers. The female has olive and yellowish plumage. Where male and female birds were so different in colour, they were frequently not even recognised as being of the same species when Agricola painted this male. It is probable that he was not aware of the yellow bird being the female. Another hundred and fifty years passed before scientists had identified the pair of most species and artists then regularly painted both the male and female together.

Crossbills live in conifer plantations being dependent on seeds, mainly of spruce, for their food. They have parrot-like actions in feeding, and use the crossed mandibles as levers to prise open tough fir cones to extract the seeds. The breeding season is closely tied to the ripening of the cones and so may occur as early as February. By late spring, family parties gather together in large flocks and roam the countryside in search of food. Their presence is often first indicated by a metallic flight call as they fly above the tree-tops. When they perch, they sidle along branches and hang from them parrot-fashion. Agricola could have been familiar with them in German forests had he been a field naturalist.

Agricola's picture of the *Crossbill* was painted when the old century gave way to a new era very different from the one in which the old masters had worked. Many of them had painted under restrictions imposed by religion. These had now been removed, but in the eighteenth century a new conflict began to emerge, this time between the demands of art and science. The problems of reconciling these demands were gradually worked out by the foremost bird artists over the next two centuries.

INDEX OF BIRDS

INDEX

Forthcoming Publications

A Dictionary of
BIRD PAINTERS OF THE WORLD

Christine E. Jackson

This is the first dictionary of bird painters of the world to be published for almost fifty years. It contains more biographical information than has hitherto been available, with many more illustrations. Approximately 5000 artists, past and present, who have made two-dimensional portraits of birds as the main motif in their paintings are included in this Dictionary, with their biographical details.

Some painted large canvases filled with birds for an imaginary earthly paradise, while others made detailed studies of a single species. Many great masters painted a bird, and the specialist bird painters knew not only how to paint feathers but also understood the birds' anatomical structure. These artists were given commissions to record newly-discovered species.

The variety of their approach is well illustrated in some 1000 colour and black and white plates. The introduction surveys varying aspects of bird portraiture by different cultures. The artists' biographies, arranged alphabetically, include comments on their individual style and achievements. A list of galleries where their work may be viewed is also included. An additional benefit of the Dictionary is that sales and auctions of bird paintings in both salerooms and galleries during the past ten years are listed, with the prices realised.

This Dictionary is a worthy addition to the long list of important art reference books published by The Antique Collectors' Club over the last twenty years.

Fable of the Raven by Pieter Casteels, 1719

When Zeus decided to appoint a king over the birds, he commanded them all to assemble on an appointed day. The raven realised how dull he looked and so he collected colourful moulted feathers from other birds and adorned himself with them. Zeus chose him to be king but the other birds, having observed his deception, indignantly stripped him of his false feathers, each one taking back his own feather. The moral is variously drawn as "men in debt cut a dash with other people's money" or "make people pay up, and you see them for the nobodies they are". (From Volume II.)

Further volumes to be published in the series

GREAT BIRD PAINTINGS OF THE WORLD

Christine E. Jackson

Volume II : The Eighteenth Century

In the early eighteenth century, several artists continued to produce bird paintings in the same style and composition as the Old Masters. When a new sensitivity to nature became universal, naturalists recorded, named and illustrated species with increasing skill and old myths were replaced by observation and evidence. This age of discovery was also a period when the full potential of watercolour painting was developed, a perfect medium for depicting birds.

Volume III : The Nineteenth Century

A century of both progression and retrogression, with the greatest achievement being the way in which the demands of art and science were reconciled within a single painting.

Volume IV : The Twentieth Century

Probably the greatest impact on bird art in this century was the emergence of some very fine North American artists. The emphasis in bird painting became the placing of the bird in its correct environment and habitat, with an excellence of drawing and realism.

Robin and Redstart by Archibald Thorburn   Courtesy Richard Green

Thorburn was one of the outstanding bird artists at work in the early years of the twentieth century. He was an excellent landscape painter and his pictures of the birds' environment suited his subjects, their colouring blending as in nature.   (From Volume IV.)

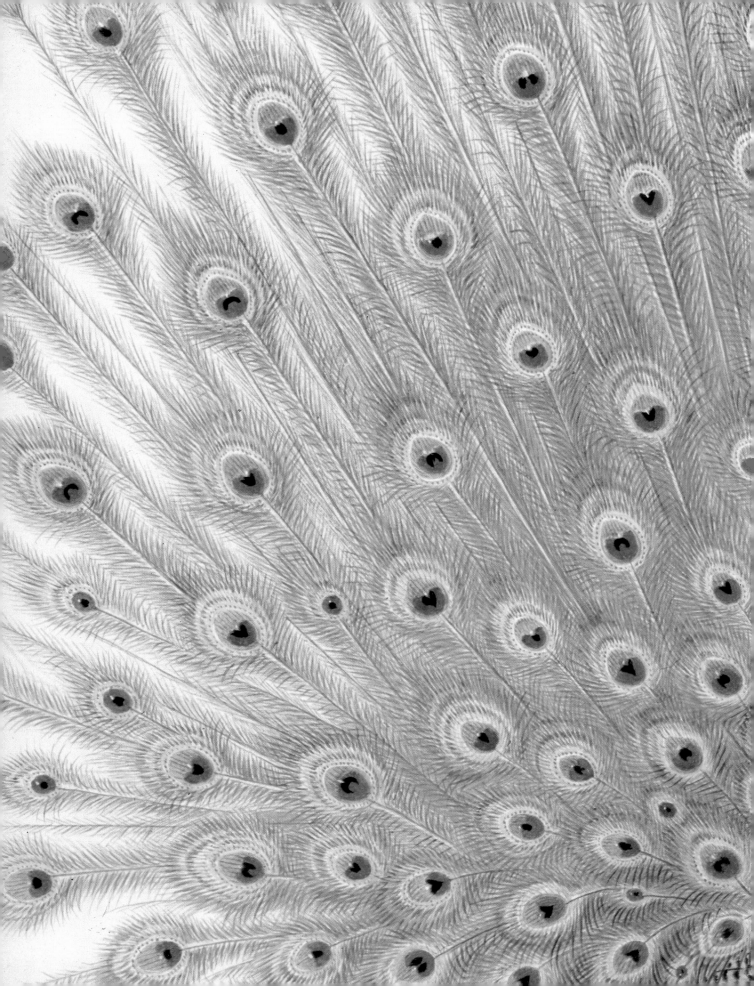